THE DOLPHIN LETTERS

VITAL INFORMATION FROM SEA TO LAND

Muriel Lindsay

Also by the author

The Chronicles of the Savannah River Dolphins

ISBN: 1-9329931120

Dedication

To all who are aware of the pull of the tides in their veins and wish to hear ocean voices

"Note from the Publisher"

As the literary agent for Eckhart Tolle, Neale Donald Walsch and many other great spiritual teachers I have often read classic books of wisdom before anyone else. This short book, THE DOLPHIN LETTERS, is such a book. You do not need to believe in dolphin communication to benefit from this book. The messages in these letters for those with higher spiritual awareness are simply pure truth. The intelligence of the Dolphins is the intelligence of the universe itself. Dolphin consciousness is superior to human consciousness at this time and a reflection from the future of where human consciousness must evolve to if we are to survive as a species. This is a book of great hope. I encourage everyone to read this book and share it with everyone you know. Just reading THE DOLPHIN LETTERS is a healing experience. For those of you who are ready, a direction is given with specific instructions of how you can become a truly global and galactic citizen and dip ever more completely into the joy aspect of creation and, more particularly, in the creation of your own life.

William Gladstone, Publisher, Waterfront Digital Press

PREFACE

Where I live now, on a barrier island off the coast of Georgia, I share the water with a large pod of dolphins. Over a 15 year period, I have gotten to know them very well and be in deep appreciation of what they bring to us. I have spent untold hours connecting with them both in the water and from a kayak, always respectful and in an open and receptive state. They have reciprocated in kind. Out of these interactions came an initial book I wrote (*The Chronicles of the Savannah River Dolphins*) about these dolphins, along with a short documentary. I knew there was more to follow about sharing what I get from them because it seems to be a large part of why I am here in this particular lifetime.

A month ago, after finding out some discouraging news about what misbegotten human ambitions are about to be wrought upon the welfare of these wonderful water beings I live with, I set out at sunset in my kayak "Buttercup" with a very heavy heart. The sun was angling down closer to the horizon and creating a play of light on the water that began to have a mesmerizing effect. There was something different about this light even though I had observed sunset light on this waterway hundreds if not thousands of times before. I could not stop gazing at it. Something shifted inside of me while the light held me captive. For no known reason, I began to feel uplifted and hopeful. It was at that point that dolphins congregated around my kayak in large numbers (they have a way of just showing up) and I took in their presence in a way new to me. I don't even remember if I spoke the words out loud or not, but I remember strongly feeling "HELP ME TO HELP YOU." It was as if they said back "OK. WE WILL."

That night, I had extensive dreams about dolphins but could not remember the details except that it felt there was a lot of compressed information. Sometime during the following day, it came to me as immediately as when Athena was born from the forehead of Zeus. I was to write a book in which I would let the dolphins make their voices known. My job, in essence, was to take dictation. I did so, and this book is the result. The whole writing took place with such grace and insistence and never once did I question why I was doing this.

How you read these letters and what you make of the source of what is written, I will leave up to you to figure out. Choose what explanation you like best. I do ask this of you. The important thing in these pages is the energy IN the messages as much as the messages themselves. Please register what becomes engendered in you. I promise you, that information will be significant.

Thank you in advance for listening to the voices behind the letters. When I read and re-read them, I feel benefitted every single time. My heartfelt hope is the same is true for you.

In service to the seas and her embodiments,

Muriel Lindsay

Table of Contents

LETTER 1

Dear Humans,

These letters are overdue. We have long been aware of wanting to share many things with you but, well, you know how it is. There are fish to catch and children to raise and so much sheer enjoyment of life to be had.

But now, we must write to you, for there comes a time when things must be said.

Let us begin with the most important message. You are ok in our book. We have observed you for millennia and we see the spark that you carry. Word has it that we dolphins delight you and make you feel good. Just so you know, the feeling is mutual and has been from the beginning of our connection with you.

Speaking of millennia, a lot of history has passed on our shared Earth. Much has transpired, not all of it pleasant, and now we find ourselves at a very particular place of planetary unfoldment. In part, this critical juncture (we consider it to be so) is why we choose to write you now.

This planet we share, ahhh . . . isn't she magnificent. When we swim, we hear her heart beat reverberating in the water. We watch the sun rise and set. We see the stars lay across us like a holy blanket. We watch clouds roll in and storms form and dissipate, all in response to this planet's churning through space.

We of the water live in a kind of reverie of amazement at life itself on this planet. Being in the water in reverie is the most natural state in the world for us. Many of your kind know what we mean, you who ride the waves, dive freely and glory in the altogether different rhythms of being on, in or under the water.

We once were land creatures and traded that in for going into the seas and rivers, and we have never looked back. We like it here.

So why are we writing you at this particular time in your history? Much hangs in the balance for everything on the planet now. Most imbalances experienced in the process of living and discovery self-correct over time. Every so often, self-correction itself, as a balancing mechanism, is in jeopardy due to a combination of factors, factors we in the sea are aware of that massively impact all of life on this planet. We are not sure you humans understand this piece, so we speak up.

It is exactly when things are the most in jeopardy that the greatest opportunity exists for something new to be born. For the "something new" to emerge, something older has to leave. In the beginning, the "something new" may appear in a form you do not recognize, nor know what to do with.

So many of you are personally transforming and doing so with a beautiful quality of light emanating from you. To observe you is like watching a star be born. We are in awe of your choice to have the courage to go into the fires of purification and to change your minds. When the law of the land has for so long been about the necessity of boundaries and hard edges of definition, it is nothing less than heroic to trust that the emanations from your own heart are all you need. To begin to make a case for this, we need to bring up the topics of death and suffering.

You humans, as a general rule, have several prominent attitudes about death. For some, if your time on Earth is mainly one of struggle, death can represent relief. It becomes almost a saving grace in a very difficult life. To others of you who like to feel you have control over events in your life, death and its association with suffering and the great unknown becomes the enemy and is to be resisted and avoided and treated as unnatural and dreaded.

For the most part, humans do not regard death as being a natural part of life in a body. Your fear of it accounts for a lot of diminishment in your lives. Death for our species is a topic we go into in more detail in another letter, so we will not elaborate on that just yet except to say we hold death in a way you might find helpful to know about.

Let us segue for a moment to the love many of you have for us for which we say to you, we feel it and it adds great value to our lives. You are very concerned for us and our welfare from many angles. You know there are those who capture and kill us and exploit us for monetary gain. You know that oil spills in the ocean have killed us and despoiled ocean environments in a horrifying way. You know that the once primarily silent seas are now flooded with levels of sound that disorient us, makes us deaf and unable to function that leads to the out right killing of us from internal hemorrhaging and beaching episodes, all in the name of creating devices for protection in times of war and sourcing more fossil fuels. Your level of upset is rising exponentially, and that very upset is stemming in part from your love for us. We understand, and as we said, we vastly appreciate your deep caring which is going to make the next thing we say sound perhaps ungrateful.

We do not want you to be upset for this damages your quality of life more than you know, but there is something we do want from you. And this is very very important. It goes back to what we were saying about the most dangerous times being the times of the greatest opportunity for bringing in something new. We want you humans to do just that . . . bring in something new. It needs to be of you and from you so we cannot be too specific about what we would recommend but we can drop some hints and will be doing so in each letter we write.

By the way, little known fact: most whales and dolphins on this planet at this time are from the future as are many people being born now. This is not a rational thought so trying to explain it would probably only serve to further confuse, but it is a thought to play with, and we dolphins are big on play, as you know.

We will bring this initial letter to a close. We have much to share but will break it up into parts and pieces. We prefer you treat each letter as a whole unto itself, and yes, there is a method in our madness.

the dolphins

LETTER 2

Dear Humans,

Here is a dolphin perspective for your consideration. Keep in mind that we dolphins are self aware and have cognitive abilities on par with, and in some cases surpassing your own, due to our evolving in the water. We do not identify with roles and yet, we do all socially that you do. We parent, we teach, we explore our individual abilities, we donate our gifts to each other, but, we do not identify with any of these expressions as being who we are. The advantage of this lack of role identification is that we do not torture ourselves with thoughts of succeeding or failing by measuring ourselves against rigid and unrelenting standards. So, we are free in the moment to respond to the needs of the moment both of the pod and of the individuals around us. For lack of a better way of putting it, we will call how we operate "pod consciousness."

If an exceptionally rambunctious dolphin needs to be reined in for his own safety and learning, any dolphin can become the momentary disciplinarian, but we hold no concept of any behavior being bad or wrong. We simply teach how energies can best be coordinated for the good of the whole. A dolphin pod could be compared to a well oiled machine but we assure you, there is nothing remotely machine-like about us. We just understand "flow", and given we have been at it for upwards of 30 million years, as your Spock would say, it is logical that we would have attained a certain level of mastery.

The simplest way to say what we mean by "flow" would be to say it refers to vividly inhabiting each moment. Go deep rather than wide. Spending time with us in actuality or in spirit will prove to become contagious, and you will find yourselves becoming better flow-ers (or flowers, if you prefer) yourselves. We need to warn you about that.

A point we would like to make here is that there is a very real way in which we are as a mirror to who you are becoming. We are showing you who you once were and will be again. Watch us long enough and a feeling of deep remembrance and familiarity will start to re-surface. How do we know this? It has something to do with that mysterious reference in the first letter about our being from the future. Just so you know, as we continue to write these letters, there are certain things you will notice keep repeating. That is quite on purpose. Repetition is a wonderful learning tool. You will only take in what belongs to you from all that we say. All else will fall away.

the dolphins

LETTER 3

Dear Humans,

We would like to speak with you about what you call the miraculous and magical, and what we experience as being just the way things work. What is required of you now, and what you are perfectly capable of doing at this time in your evolution is tantamount to what many of you would think of as impossible. It is not. It just takes a timely leap. On one side of the chasm which you will feel called upon to leap over, you will feel only a miracle could take you across. But once on the other side, you will simply feel: "of course." Your beautiful spirit in human form named Nik Wallenda, when he walked on a cable across the Grand Canyon, did that for all of humanity, that you might upgrade your belief of your own abilities to have courage and faith and do what seems just too hard.

You humans hold such a special place on the planet having to do with the way you have been evolving your consciousness. You have been on an awesomely difficult journey and yet, you are still here, and you have evolved, but you have not done so in an even way.

You have gone through stages of learning, of doing and then over-doing. You then return to the drawing board and dedicate yourself to finding a new balance point. Taking these kinds of evolutionary steps can take millennia.

Right now, you are in the middle of a crucial need for re-balance due to your tendency to over-do. Part of why you get into trouble is also part of your beauty. Your enthusiasm for something is so great that a momentum occurs and then it is hard to put the brakes on. Sometimes you even forget what the original impetus was to pursue a certain course, but you perpetuate it with vigor all the same.

Much of your self-judgment about what you are doing "wrong" comes from your not seeing the Big Picture of what the process of evolving consciousness entails. The horrors you have visited and created in your own over enthusiasm for steaming ahead faster than you can assimilate causes you to feel badly about yourselves, either consciously or unconsciously.

One reason we are here writing you is to help you to understand why we do not resist your acts of misguidedness where our welfare is concerned. We know you do not deserve to be hated. The acts you do in ignorance do have repercussions and must be addressed but can only successfully be done so when you find a way to see yourselves like we see you, see the beauty of your spirit. Right now, because of imbalances perpetuated on this Earth, your overall beauty of spirit is not as obvious, but we see it. We know who you were and will be again and our intention with you is to show you perspectives you may be unaccustomed to having.

Much of your creativity teaches us. We marvel at the range of your abilities. We want to learn from you. But first things first. We cannot collaborate if our home, the water, is not protected. It is a huge paradox. Until you let go of your self-dislike and even in some cases, self-hatred (again, be it conscious or unconscious), you will not be able to value your world of which we are a part. If we go, then our ability to help you learn a new perspective about your true beauty also goes. The last thing we would ever want to do is make you feel badly about your essential being, and, it is important that we get your attention about the pre-eminent need for course correction on this planet. You have such an opportunity to amaze yourselves. We can help you forgive yourselves if that issue becomes a blockage even though we honestly hold nothing against you.

There are some dolphins and whales in unacceptable conditions who do despair, but on the whole, we only see possibility for the best of humanity to evolve here and now when it is most needed. Collaboration of land and sea beings is available like never before.

You can come up with ideas we have no concept of. We are greatly anticipating being surprised in the best of ways by you. And, there are no guarantees if the opportunities we are sharing in this time of creative potential on this beautiful Earth are not apprehended.

The only way to grab these opportunities is for you humans to develop a new regard for who you are and why you are here and then for you to experience what is meant by self love. Truly, your developing self love is the ONLY way. Somewhere inside you remember this.

The Garden of Eden represents the state of un-self-conscious but no less tangible self love. You may think Eden was a place that existed on Earth, or you may think it is a myth. We suggest it is a memory of connection with who you are with where you come from.

No-one kicked anyone out of "heaven on Earth." There was a message given to humankind though that said: "Go explore, but remember to come back." It is now time to come back. To a large degree, we dolphins went and explored too, but we perhaps remember the way back a little more clearly than you do for we went less far afield.

Something very large is wanting our joint creation, yours and ours. It is just waiting to be born. We are aware of how strongly, in our letters to you, we are driving this point home about our collaborating with you. It is a point we choose to make from as many angles as possible to assist you to connect the dots with what we are offering. We swim to you in these letters like we swim in the water. We look like we are all over the place, but we know exactly what we are doing.

the dolphins

LETTER 4

Dear Humans,

It's not too late. Many of you are aware of the issues on this planet that seem overwhelming and irreversible. You feel there are too many of you. You have been in the midst of much damage to the planet herself and to each other. Religious extremism continues to create war and death. Children still go hungry. Refugee camps replace what was home. Things are being done to animal species, the rainforest and seas that will take potentially thousands of years to correct. Slavery still exists. Radiation looms as a threat. Greed is rampant. Most of your governments are inefficient and some of them corrupt in the extreme. The list goes on. Even though we have done nothing to contribute to these societal ills, we too are suffering the effects. We just painted a grim picture, so how can we say it is not too late?

We can because we have been on this planet for 30 million years. We have witnessed all manners of destruction and periods of having to virtually start over. And guess what. This marvelous ball of dirt we share knows how to recover. She has done so many times, but each time she does, it takes what it takes. There have never been this many people on the planet before so that does somewhat change the equation.

What has to happen to right our listing earthship has not happened yet, but it is beginning to happen. There are many signs indicating so, but you must look for them. May we share an analogy? There is a phenomenon in the seas that happens at a certain time of year on a full moon. Corals release many millions of spores that will in turn serve to reproduce more coral. At first, you just see a few spores, then more and finally, a flood of them.

You humans can be likened to this flood of spores. What needs to happen is for humans to take a leap to deciding about all of Life from a place of deep feeling that is not attached to a belief. When you do, the end result is a marvelous state within yourself, a kind of fellow feeling or, in dolphin speak, a pod feeling. It is what you let yourself experience when you fall in love. We dolphins live in that place and do not reserve that feeling for one special other. No, we are not monogamous but we are honest and loyal to the greater good, and it would not occur to us to downplay the significance of our feeling nature. We run on it. Our intelligence is in service to it.

You seem, from what we understand, aware of our cognitive abilities, but you need to know we feel everything intensely. We do not use our intelligence to hold beliefs that end up curtailing our abilities to fully open to the moment of what is going on around us.

Beliefs are often turned into gods by your species. Why do you need them? Can you conceive of life without them? What do you think will happen if you change your mind about the importance of beliefs? Would you quit feeling passionate? Or quit caring? Would you lose your bearings and no longer know who you are? We suggest that letting go of a set of beliefs is exactly when things start to get really interesting, and they stay that way. We know because that is how we live. That is why we love you no matter what you do to us because we don't hold a belief that you are wrong. We know you are where you are and we can detect how you are getting in your own way, but that is just awareness on our part, and not belief.

We see you as a naturally open system here to interact with all of creation just like we are. Your potential is as available and natural to your evolving as ours is to us. Our great joy is the discovery of what we can create just out of ourselves and from our beingness. We see that same quality in many of you. We also see many of you so hemmed in by your beliefs that your freedom to explore your potential is greatly limited. We also know all this limitation can change in a heartbeat, and when that happens to large numbers of people, you will become like the millions of spores releasing under a full moon that one night out of the year. The explosion of creativity from your kind will be like nothing this world has seen while you have graced her with your presence. We rejoice at this prospect. This is why we could never and will never give up on your ability to shift in the needed ways. It is also why we are writing to mirror to you your potential for true freedom and health and balance. Giving up on you would be like our giving up on ourselves, which is virtually impossible, for we are not bound. You might want to re-read this last sentence, for it is saying ever so much.

the dolphins

LETTER 5

Dear Humans,

You sometimes wonder about us and our awareness of what is above us, the stars, phases of the moon, eclipses and other heavenly phenomena. Yes, we are aware and observe such things with interest and curiosity. We are always looking for new ways to relate to what is above us, around us and below us. We notice land phenomena as well. Sometimes we lay our heads sidewise on the water to look up at the skies and just gaze. We ponder not so much in thought as in feeling what is stirred within. We register how the energies within us are moved. This is our primary modality for deriving understanding of experience. One way to describe this would be to say we are aware always of vibration, within and without, and the different forms it takes as in the wavelengths of light, color and sound. Being informed by the nuances of vibration is our specialty.

You humans are interested in communicating with us in ways that might be compared to learning another's language. That is not how it works. You and we will learn how to communicate by using "a third thing" other than the spoken word or analyzing our sounds. Our sounds do hold meaning and there is nothing wrong with your undertaking to "crack the code" but our real connecting will occur in another manner. As you continue reading our letters, the dots will start connecting more.

Returning to the topic of our awareness of what goes on in the night skies or even in the day for that matter, let us say this. Our connectivity to the environment is so complete that very little escapes us. Yes, we can be momentarily distracted and bump into a boat. Yes, we can end up in harm's way when dolphin capturing is going on, which raises huge questions about our intelligence. We are susceptible to disorientation just like you are and the way we are captured insures we are disoriented first. Our point here is to share that we are exceedingly open to all inner and outer cues due to the state we have evolved to in which we have the freedom to just be ourselves even as, like you, we are becoming more. This very freedom is so much of what we wish to emphasize in these letters, for humanity at large does not yet have it to our degree, but it awaits you. But we digress.

Returning to the topic of what do we make of the moon and the stars and other sky phenomena, we are very affected and reminded of the fact that we are on a planet and on an earthly dimension but we are also in space and in other dimensions simultaneously. "Dimensions" here refer to certain strata of our feeling natures and relate to vibrational shifts which we have indicated is what we attend to most of all. Our specialties can all be learned and developed by you, through your consciousness and its exponentially developing capacities. The night sky and sunrise and sunset in particular provide doorways for you to enter the greater realms of your being, and we are now in a time when you must do that. It is required so that you may operate in a different way than you have before, at least on a mass level. It used to be an option to take this evolutionary step forward. Now it is a necessity. That is another reason we are writing to you at this juncture. We know that the portals of the sky are opening. For that reason, and for their sheer beauty, we like to gaze up and indulge in a state of remembrance.

Just to keep it interesting, for us, memory is not just about the past. It is simply about expanding our awareness of who we are. We get bigger, so to speak, when remembrance vibrates within us. Expansion is our destiny, and it is yours as well.

the dolphins

LETTER 6

Dear Humans,

We would like to speak to you about the perceived violence in Nature and the way, for example, much of life does not seem to survive its early beginnings. An example would be the birth of sea turtles and the march of hundreds of hatchlings up and out of the sand to the sea. Many of these young ones do not even make it to the water because they are caught by predators before they get that far. The ones who do make it to the water still have to contend with many miles of strong ocean currents and more predators before they get to the relative safety of the sea grasses. For the especially tender hearted of your species, this drama of life and early death seems sad and almost cruel. You identify with what you imagine is the helplessness the hatchling must feel. In turn, this can have the effect of causing you to look at Nature with a somewhat distrustful and baleful eye. It can set up a sense of separation as if you and Nature are playing by a different set of rules for, as a creator of life, you would want to give the young and helpless better odds.

We have a different take on the matter. First of all, we are Nature. We know that the life that runs through all forms is the same as the life that runs through us. Though we are cognitive beings and have higher thought processes, as do you, we use ours differently. It has something to do with living in the water. We believe in aligning with the currents of life. We do not hang out with notions of good and bad (though we do know what we like). To us, life is just what is happening for us to experience and grow and learn from. We respond with excitement when the fish are plentiful, and we feel emotion when something happens to a pod member but are not drawing conclusions about what should be.

Emotions for us consist of strong currents in our body, the same as with you. We respond to our emotions differently. We feel what we feel profoundly and completely, always in response to what is going on in the moment. Do we jump out of the moment and anticipate things based on past experiences? Not like you do. We are great synthesizers in life so we can take a huge amount of information in during any given moment, using all of our evolved aspects and create a balance in our individual bodies, minds and spirits and in our pod. We are so fully engaged in this manner of living that anticipating or harking back offers us little.

What we are saying is, to us, life is a multi-layered experience of the moment we are in that does not require us to draw conclusions about the equity of things. You humans spend much time in deep thought on matters such as why are things the way they are when you would prefer they be otherwise. We don't do that not because we cannot, but because our evolution has brought us to a place of accepting the moment completely in order to fully experience life. This includes unhappy endings or, we should say, outcomes in which, like you, our hearts break a little or a lot. We understand that, in the Bigger Picture, it makes sense. You will too. That we can promise you. Expanding consciousness gives us that grace.

One reason we do not linger in sorrow is because life keeps giving her gifts. Under circumstances of utter misery, dolphins have been known to go into despair and even to commit suicide, which is relatively easy to do because our breath is not automatic like yours is. We choose every breath we take.

What you need to know is we do not suffer about our suffering. Well we know we are not just here on this planet for ourselves. We are here for the whole. It is one reason we do so well as a pod. We have learned that altruism and self love is the same thing so we don't personalize much of anything.

Yes, our cousins, the orcas lashed out at human trainers (though we suggest a distinction here that dolphins and orcas are not subject to being trained but rather they decide to give humans what they want). When the frustration of being in thwarting conditions (such as in a small area of concrete) becomes overwhelmingly intolerable, that is when the lashing out has occurred in the few instances that it has. You must know of the inordinate amount of forbearance many of these captive dolphins and whales practice for years on end. Do our kind and your kind form affectionate bonds under these circumstances of captivity? Yes, but the humans would be shocked to learn that often what is at the base of the affection is pity for them. There are exceptions having to do with something you have labeled "dolphin assisted therapy" but we will save that for another time.

The bottom line is that we are better at non-resistance than you have become yet. To you, non-resistance in the face of what you have decided is wrong and should not be in the first place feels off the mark, like you are giving sanction to what you do not want. That assessment, in and of itself locks down much or your creative potential.

We dolphins do not use pain to evolve ourselves. We use life itself and profound interest in it and love of it to evolve, and what that requires is to not resist the forms life is taking so much as to find a way to flow with them much as you practice in some of your martial arts. You are capable of evolving out of love and interest and not using pain as the primary means but most of you do not believe that. For one thing, you do not trust you are good enough to deserve to live in that kind of world. One of our strongest messages to you is to observe how we dolphins do evolve primarily based on the positives of the gift of life. We are passionate about getting you humans on board with this understanding of possibility. You are right on the brink of getting it, certain ones of you. There will be a tremendous domino effect once the "create just out of the joy of it" starts catching on for real and quits being too good to be true.

Globally, things look very dark and forbidding now because you are right on the brink of a breakthrough. There is great mystery in all of this and we do encourage you to use your higher intellectual faculties to ponder what we say here. Nothing less than the freedom to come into the fullness of your being is at stake, something each of you wants with all your heart even if you don't dwell on it.

the dolphins

LETTER 7

Dear Humans,

To help make our case for the significance of our connections with you, we would like to give you a symbolic example. It is one of those things that mean more when you let it "settle" into your awareness. Both humans and dolphins enjoy the domains of air and that of water. You are mostly in air and visit water. We are mostly in water and visit air. There is an activity we both enjoy that is the reverse of each other. We dolphins love to get up a head of steam and burst high up into the air and then of course, fall back into the water. You, on the other hand, love to run to the end of the diving board or the edge of a cliff and plunge into the water with great velocity which takes you deep, but then you return to air. We are mirroring each other. We feel it is important you begin to notice the way this is true, about the mirroring, not just because it is interesting but because it is a significant piece of discovering more about our connection. We have pieces you need and you have pieces we need and the whole planet stands to gain by these discoveries. It is more than metaphor to say we are the yin to your yang, or that water is the yin to the yang of land and air-based living.

The most important thing of all is what you discover and uncover from your own inspiration. Our intent with you for millennia has been to inspire you so that you may know more of your creative potency. When we refer to your creativity, we also include in that the need for balance, and not going overboard in any direction without correcting things in short order. We can tell by looking at your fields of energy, which we can easily see, how things are going with you. The degree to which we trust our feeling nature is what allows us to do this since that is our top priority, and has been the most prominent aspect on our evolutionary path. You have amongst yourself the "sensitives"–that is, humans who can also do these things. So we and the sensitives among you know when you are being open to your creative potential and when you are out of balance and so not as open. Word of advice, don't ever try to fool a dolphin. You won't succeed. True, there are methods of capturing us that in effect fool us because the methods used create massive disorientation in our sensitive sound-discerning capabilities. It is not playing fair, for sure, but playing fair is an ethical consideration and, as in the case of any kind of slavery, is usually perpetuated by not being willing to assess the equality of the ones being enslaved with yourselves. There is always justification for the action, and taking those actions dims your own light, not because you are being evil, but because you are being blind to a greater perspective.

We understand that at present, the playing field is very uneven among the evolutions of different people who are all part of the human family, with some being more, shall we say, ahead of the game. Those of you who can read what we share with you in these letters, and feel what is behind the words, are among the ones who are going to tip the balance. Things do appear to get worse off-times before they get better, during such mutating times as these but we encourage you to not pause in your creative enthusiasms just because others are mired in what needs to be released. You cannot save anyone from their chosen path but you can most assuredly inspire others to save themselves. You inspire us when we see your light. You most certainly do that.

the dolphins

LETTER 8

Dear Humans,

Let's talk about war. Most people think of war as being caused by a battle of belief systems, which is a topic we have already addressed somewhat. War is often about boundaries, drawing lines of separation and having issues of ownership, territoriality, if you will. Many in the animal kingdom are very territorial. Even plants can battle each other over territory. So it would seem that territoriality is part of life on planet Earth.

Under the sea, battles also rage over territory. Even crustaceans get in on it. But there is something we dolphins know and practice for the most part, and it goes something like this. We are in a body that has needs, but we are not that body. We are the spirit inhabiting the body. Yes, if fish are scarce, we can get very food focused, but we treat life more like a game, an adventure, a mystery.

Our consciousness is spiritually aligned in that we do know that we are first and foremost spiritual beings. Most people have no idea an animal, even a very smart animal, would have that perspective. Some recognize the expansion of our consciousness and then exalt us into being angels or magical beings, in the mythical sense. We are magical, but no more so than you humans are though you do not usually think of yourselves that way. When we refer to magical, we just mean aligning with the natural world, the importance of which is so much behind our messages to you in these letters. When we are made out to be "magical beings" by those who ascribe many things to us, this goes beyond what magic really is and creates distortions.

The point we are making here is a tendency for humans to not recognize who we are or, to go into the other direction of making us more than we are. We are as your older siblings. Our life styles, so to speak, and resulting capabilities are different since, as you know, one's environment has a strong shaping effect. And there is that matter of our having been here 25 million years longer than you have which has given us more time to work out many things.

Living in the water greatly reduces any tendency we might have towards territoriality. Part of the evolution of our consciousness has to do with an understanding of the concept of "flow"–the natural movement of energies in the Universe, and a concomitant understanding that optimal flow benefits all. When you resist nothing, you are in the flow, which again brings up the martial arts comparison.

One reason we dolphins do not resist being captured and killed is because we don't just flow with small currents. We are capable of, as a pod consciousness, from time to time, flowing with the currents of the Big Picture when it becomes apparent that none are free until all are free. So we allow certain things to be perpetrated upon us so that more might awaken. We are not martyrs and have no desire to give up our joyous existence but when the flow takes us into harm's way, our tendency is to follow the lead of what we consider to be the Intelligence behind all life.

In truth, some of the wars you humans have engaged in have been part of a flow as well. A flow that you partly engineered through your choices and yet a flow that had a side effect of breaking your hearts open with compassion where perhaps none existed before.

We encourage you not to judge your own history. What is done is done, but now, this moment in time is different. A window of opportunity is here that is too good to pass up. We would even go so far as to say, in an overall way, it would be dangerous to pass it up. We write to you to give you a nudge, but always with appreciation for who you really are if you could only see yourselves as we see you. We will never give up on you until there is nothing left, and there is no reason things need to come to that. We have no desire to scare you. You are eternal beings no matter what, as are we, but this sphere we share called Earth or Gaia is a being who cannot and will not sustain certain practices. So if we wish to continue sharing her, we need to collaborate.

How do we do that, you may ask. We have many ideas about how to do that, but first, we needed to have the attention of enough of you. It is no accident that you are reading these letters. There are more words out there than ever before, all vying for your attention. That you are attending to these words is a message from you to you, for humans who are sufficiently awake are very guided as to what they do, who they are with and what they pay attention to. That guidance is not only helpful, it assists in making your current life quite the adventure. Even those you might think of as suffering due to their circumstances, if they choose to expand their awareness might surprise you with their having an attitude of their life being an adventure of self discovery. Some of these circumstantially limited ones, such as your Mr.Nelson Mandela while he was in prison, could be the very ones who are able to break through limitations holding humanity back, for they have had a lot of practice and a chance to go deeper within their own consciousness and be more open to what is trying to be born. We see this situation in places all over the globe and it lets us know that mass collaboration between our species is drawing closer.

the dolphins

LETTER 9

Dear Humans,

Some of you are concerned about bringing children into this world during this time of so much chaos. Even as you detect that the chaos is in service of bringing in a higher order, you still feel unsure. You are aware of the hardships worldwide that children are having to endure. Your heart clinches at the thought of bringing a child into this world in love and out of love and subjecting them to the unknown aspects of this century.

We suggest to you that the souls who would come through you want to be here and take their chances. Certainly do not bring in a child if you do not want to, but if you do want to and feel your life is structured to support that, then know this. You are doing the child a favor.

All of you know what you are getting into before you enter this world though you forget shortly after you are born. Regarding the birth of a child, the single most important feature is that the child is wanted. . .not wanted to complete the parent, but wanted for the joy of creating, then serving the creation, and finally, being re-made in that service.

When a dolphin baby is born, all the generations of females in the pod gather round. The young one comes into a circle of love that never goes away. Extended families in the human race still happen, but are not a given. The smaller the circle in a family, the more stress on the parents and fear of being overwhelmed by all the unknowns they will be dealing with in bringing up children.

The drives to be an individual and to equally feel a part of the whole is not something most humans have learned to coordinate. The tendency is to lean towards one of these two more than the other. This is where we come in. We have amalgamated treasuring individuality and membership in the pod equally. Remember "the third thing" we mentioned? This amalgamation is one example of it. As you spend more time with us, observing us and feeling us, how this amalgamation can occur is something you can learn, we almost want to say, by osmosis. This particular "third thing" is integrally related to our experience of freedom. The reasons why that is will become increasingly apparent to you. We will not say too much more about what we mean just yet. Discovery is such a joy and we would not for the world take it away from you. That is why we like to say, we are just dropping hints. Helpful ones, we hope.

the dolphins

LETTER 10

Dear Humans,

Today we would like to write about the topic of knowledge. We have two questions for you. How do you know what you know, and how do you know that you know? And then, we ask how has your knowledge served you? Knowledge is so basic to life that for most humans, it seems to be a given, like breathing air, and not in need of looking at any deeper than that. You have spent millennia developing your brain and its capacity for thought and logic and language and concepts. This is how you have come to where you are in your evolution.

We bring this up to share with you a contrast from an equally evolved brain so that you may stretch and participate in creating another "third thing." We dolphins come to "know" differently than you. A better way to describe our relationship with knowledge is that we "recognize." Think of a kaleidoscope and how, when you twist it, a whole other pattern emerges. Our relationship with massive input from currents of energy is constantly, in the moment, showing us new potential. We "recognize" what the potential is and this becomes our knowledge, in that very moment. Living so acutely in the moment, do we accumulate information or does our "knowledge" dissipate as soon as it is born? We do not hold on to anything out of fear of loss. Just as when we exhale, we release all air completely–what belongs to one moment is released as we open to the next moment. But if you observe us from the outside, you will see an almost seamless flow from moment to moment. We have no need to accumulate or hold on to anything because the moment supplies all our needs. To you humans, this seems almost incomprehensible. And yes, our neurology is always upgrading with added experience. We ourselves, as beings, become the books of knowledge.

In a way, we dolphins are more innately pragmatic than you humans. We constantly adhere to the guidelines of stability, balance and harmony of the whole of which we are each a part. You humans are so remarkably creative (in ways we greatly admire, like figuring out how to get to the moon), but you have fewer checks and balances. Therefore, under the gift of free will, you are allowed to take creativity into expressions that create imbalances. We always come back to why we are writing to you at this time. It is because the imbalances now are more dangerous to the whole of humanity and to overall life on this planet than ever before. It is time to make a shift, and push has come to shove.

The next evolutionary step is to become a global village and, there is massive fear and resistance from certain quarters because of your adherence to what you think you "know." To stretch and come to regard "recognizing" as an alternate means of knowing is something more and more people are coming to experience. One way to help explain the distinction is to refer to the "field" of energy around each and every one of you and what happens in that field when you respond from your profound feeling nature without the need to label anything. We suggest to you that the most meaning in your life comes from the deepening into the nuances of feeling. Gathering knowledge has its own sense of reward for you, but it is a vulnerable reward because walking in lockstep with it is the need to be right and hold on to that. As we look at your electromagnetic field, which we do with ease because of being more cosmonauts of energy expressions than anything else, we can see the impact on your overall being by your choices and your focuses.

You have your beautiful scientists, and they are beautiful, who have learned much of what we refer to here in speaking of "fields" and can speak to you in ways that please your intellect. You likewise have among you very evolved mystics that simply radiate what we speak of. Their radiation or "shakti" as it is sometimes called, activates your nervous system and higher centers in ways similar to what we do in your presence, all having to do with your readiness to expand.

The stretching to include a different kind of ability to come to "know" is not something you have to control or make happen. We add here a simple sharing, and that is to ask you to be aware, from inside of yourself, of when you come to know by simply recognizing and valuing the amazing synthesis of all the elements in the moment that your feeling nature feeds back to you, when you pay attention. It is the simplest thing to do of all and the easiest to override in your habits of adhering to your need to accumulate what you think you know. Where you are going, well the "simple" is going to get you there.

the dolphins

LETTER 11

Dear Humans,

Are mermaids real? Do they exist in third dimension? Other dimensions (including mythological)? Do they travel between dimensions? If they do exist in our actual oceans, are they under threat by humankind and this is one reason they stay hidden?

Why is this topic showing up in your world in a big enough way to make us want to address it? We are here to share our perspective, not to convince you of anything you do not already resonate with, even if you are not totally conscious that you do. We could make a case for that we understand more of who you are as whole beings than perhaps you do yourselves. We say this not from any sort of superiority but coming from having been on this planet for a very deep time. Yes, we meant to say "deep" instead of "long" because consciousness is more about layers than it is about linear time. But we digress.

The awareness of merpeople, male and female, is significant and timely. For the anthropologists among you, there are rock carvings indicating their existence with us dolphins along with humans on land.

It is a wonderful thing when an awareness of expanded realities begins to peek through and stir the imaginations of many humans all over the globe. There will come a time when humanity is evolved enough that fear will not result from such expansions, but just from the joy of adventure. This is what humankind is on the brink of being able to do "en masse" if, and it is a big if, enough of you master your fear (much of which comes from judging yourself and anticipating punishment).

If merpeople do exist, if you make a space in your awareness for them to, then you need to know as things stand with the increase of deadly levels of sound in the ocean by humans pursuing the natural trajectory of certain beliefs they adhere to, the merpeople are in jeopardy as well as our own kind. Dolphins and whales are prepared to accept the effects of human choices, whatever they are, because that is what our consciousness decides for us. But a race you perhaps knew nothing about may have a harder go of it.

Here is what we say about "recognizing" comes into play. If you recognize a resonant feeling about the topic of merpeople, this resonance is not coming from your mind and your fund of knowledge which would consider the notion of merpeople suspect and outlandish, fairy tales, if you will. Resonance comes from the field of the heart. The French have a saying that the heart has reason that reason itself does not comprehend.

As it turns out, the most important question about merpeople is not is it true or not that they exist or have existed in our oceans. The best question is, what happens to you when you feel into the possibility of their existence. Let that reverberate, and then ride that wave. It can take you into places you can feel even if you cannot name them.

Deepening your feeling nature is that which we are here to encourage you to do in any and all ways so bear with us as we continue to drive that point home.

the dolphins

LETTER 12

Dear Humans,

In these letters, we point out contrasts between your species and our own, but in this letter, we would like to share something we have in common. Of all species, yours and ours keep our young with us among the longest periods of time. In both cases, the likely reason has to do with the complexity of our brains and the need to pass on to the young as many teachings as possible about how to navigate with such a brain.

They say to whom much is given, much is required. Your kind and our kind have been given much indeed. The gift is a great benefit and at times can be felt as a pretty crushing responsibility. Let us assure you that, from our perspective, our two species were made for handling whatever challenges life presents, utilizing our great capacities. We can not just handle things but can handle them with excellence when we take advantage of the potential.

Because of sharing this status in life of bearing a similarly endowed seat of genius, we stand to gain so much by our proximity and mutual interest in each other. Together, our shared capacities will make it possible for us to give back to life in a bigger way than we can do separately. It is a fine, fine thing that we share this planet.

the dolphins

LETTER 13

Dear Humans,

When we dolphins breathe, we exhale quickly and completely. Except for athletes and those who study and understand the power of breath, many humans tend to breathe in a haphazard way. For one thing, most humans do not completely exhale at the end of a breath so they retain carbon dioxide in the bottom of the lungs which means there is less room for new air to come in.

The reason we bring this topic up is that the way you breathe is like a metaphor. Breath is life itself. When you fully breathe, you fully live. When you completely empty your lungs at the end of a breath, you fully release what is past which in turn lands you into the present moment, which is where we dolphins reside just as a matter of course.

We understand that you already know all this theoretically but here is where our longer time of evolving gives us an edge. You could almost say, completely exhaling is a habit we developed so that we do not have to surface for air more frequently. It is the most efficient way to do things but is also in service of how we feel about life in a body. To address that, we direct you to a difference in the way two air breathers, you and us, have evolved.

Humans breathe automatically. We, on the other hand, choose every breath we take. This distinction has many ramifications. How might it change things for you to decide each time you took a breath to do so. It is a very different way to do life because it puts you in a position of being constantly aware. That may sound exhausting and like a less evolved position in which a function cannot just become secondary and automatic, but it is the breath we are talking about here, the means by which the spirit of life enters the cells of matter which have no life of their own without spirit.

We never respond to life without awareness that it is the spirit that keeps us going. By the way we breathe, we are choosing life over and over and never taking it for granted. This is the basis of so much about who we are.

One last point to be made here, think about the joy of an athlete when they are "in the zone." These are the times when they are breathing fully, exhaling fully, being fully in the moment with no concern about past or future. Whatever their innate and trained skills are can now come into expression with ease. They are, if you will forgive our presumption here, being land dolphins. They are able to balance body, mind and spirit and be completely in the flow.

This is what is going on when we do our synchronous jumps. Being in this state makes for very joyful living, and has nothing to do with accomplishing anything or competing. It is simply claiming what belongs to you, and breath is the giver of this constant gift of Life.

the dolphins

LETTER 14

Dear Humans,

What is it like to live in the water? For those of you who spend time in this world, you know it is a very dream-like realm. It alters anyone, dolphin or human, to spend time in this blue world. To a very large degree, living in water accounts for the differences in brain evolution and in priorities between our two species.

Things are more fluid in our world, both literally and figuratively, so it is harder to get stuck in positions or beliefs. We become like the ocean currents themselves, surrendering to what presents in the moment and finding our way through doing that.

Being on land and dealing with gravity can give you a sense of always needing to make an effort to get things to happen. You, in your ingenuity, have found ways to lighten up, even in the heaviness of life on land. You do this when you laugh, when you meditate, and when you find the sweet spot in any physical activity such that what you do feels effortless and time seems to stop.

For us though, we have not needed to develop a way to lighten up. It is the gift that comes with time spent under the water. Having said all this, we have a secret to share. We actually enjoy the fleeting effects of gravity when we leap into the air. It is a welcome contrast to what we are used to.

If we had not gone back into the sea and had stayed as a land mammal, our evolution, though just as long, would not have gotten us to where we are. But we did return to the sea and stayed there which gives us a perspective that now, of all times, we are very intent on sharing with you because we see you as being on the brink of something big in your own evolution. It excites us to witness such potential and it encourages us to assist you in keeping the faith when so much is collapsing, because it needs to.

If you find yourself faltering and buying too hard what the part of your brain that creates fear is selling, we have one word for you. Water. The blessing of water. Being on it, in it, drinking it, bathing in it and listening to it. Doing these things will remind you of a feeling of safety and well being and out of that, your life will turn events that could be your undoing into a sense of adventure, and that, we would suggest, is a good use of your time in a body.

the dolphins

"Pacino" - my first real dolphin friend and teacher of dolphin ways whom I have now been connected with for 12 years

a friend keeping me and my kayak "Buttercup" company

Sunset shenanigans

"Wait for me!"

Major cavorting

Nudging "Buttercup"

Sticking close to Mom

On the run

The sea - best playground ever

Swimming with and sharing sun path with a dolphin

Dolphin underfoot

Synchronized swimming

That look

My collaborators

Weaving the dark and the Light

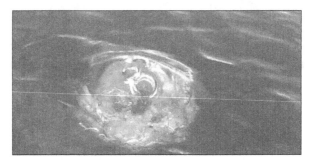

Bubble communication - dolphins have
been doing this the whole time!

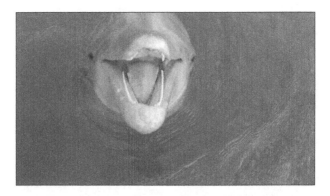

A dolphin who showed up for video as I sang happy
birthday to a friend . . . hence now called
the birthday dolphin

I get to feel what the dolphins feel being close
to the large ships

LETTER 15

Dear Humans.

In this letter, we wish to speak of what goes on when you are asleep. What happens to your consciousness while you are sleeping is a far more interesting landscape than is commonly suspected. Before going into this topic further, in answer to your wondering, yes, we dolphins do sleep, sort of. We cannot fully sleep because we are conscious breathers, but what we do is more of a blending of your versions of sleep and wakefulness and dreaming. We rest parts of our brain while keeping other parts awake. Our intention in this letter though is not to focus on how we do things.

During your sleep, you humans dream, and dream you must, for it is a means of sorting out what goes on in wakefulness. You have those who remember dreams regularly, and those who do not. You have those who pay attention to dreams and work with understanding them, and those who ignore them. We suggest to you that lumping all your nighttime memories and experiences under the one heading of "dreams" greatly oversimplifies the range of experiences your soul is giving to you. While you sleep, you are going through a virtual symphony of brain wave changes. Many portals and layers and levels are being opened to you beyond your imagining.

Many of you, children and adults alike, are visited by dolphins and whales in your sleep. It is in the night that we can find the means to reach you, communicate with you and share how we feel about you. Many of you who feel a strong bond with us do so without having spent physical time with us. Rather, you have invited us in while you slumbered in a body. While your body slows down in deep slumber, your consciousness flings open its doors of perception.

The power of these exchanges between you and us while you sleep can be just as evocative of a deep response on your part as when you are with us in the flesh. Many of you changed the course of your lives because of an encounter with our kind in the night time ethers.

Know that when we do appear in this manner, it is always to give you something. It may be to give you love or acceptance or to alert you to something that would be good for you to open up to. We are good beacons - bringing Light and pointing it in a specific direction.

Can you call us in to visit you before you go to sleep? You can, but in general, we show up based on things going on with you that you are not necessarily aware of. This means, we tend to show up when you do not expect us.

Telling you these things comes dangerously close to indicating we are your angels. It is much more apt to think of us as a caring elder sibling. When you idealize us, then you can no longer be open to us as fully because you are imposing something between us and it is confusing your understanding. Whatever your tendency is to see us as special, our request is that you discipline yourself to see us as no more special than yourselves. True, we live according to a different code in relationship to Earth herself but you are in the middle of a massive course correction and now is not the time to judge anything about yourself historically. You cannot get to where you are going without dropping the judgment. Feeling remorseful is a beautiful emotion for it means you have seen the error of your ways but once you do, look at us looking at you and seeing your Light, for we surely do, and always have.

the dolphins

LETTER 16

Dear Humans,

There are many theories abounding by humans who are interested in the ways dolphins are considered to be natural healers. We wish to address this topic for several reasons. One is, we love you as family on this planet. We admire you and wish to assist you in the ways we are capable of. Another reason is, we wish to pierce through exaggerations of what we bring to the table.

We do have the capacity to use sonar in remarkable ways, to see through so-called solid material (from a physics standpoint, material is anything but solid) and to affect vibration already existing in the energy fields with the vibration of sonar itself. This is a very generalized way to speak of these things but we trust you to accept our choice to speak simply. Go to your scientists and mystics for the particulars.

We dolphins are not only familiar with ocean waves and currents but equally as familiar with the waves and currents we swim in when we share the energy fields with others and the environment. Navigating in the realm of constantly moving energy vibrations is our specialty, so to speak, which we have alluded to before. Human science measures and identifies what it studies and is always breaking new ground in its understanding of the world of phenomena but we suggest that there remains much that is perceived within the realm of deep feeling that moves beyond being measurable by external means.

The "sensitives" among you are very similar to us in that you have great capacity to feel into the fields of energy you find yourselves in, but you do not always know what to make of what you feel. To you, we recommend that you keep diving more deeply into your feeling natures and from those depths, the answers will come.

Those of you who are natural healers, and you know who you are, do much the same as we do. You balance energies both within yourself and then in inter-activity with others. The most rigorous training for natural healers is the first part, balancing their inner energies which has to do with all they are open to from all the dimensions. This can take decades of learning because they frequently have to learn from trial and error. When they do reach a strong stable balancing mechanism within themselves (almost gyroscopic in nature), we consider them to be a kind of land dolphin.

It is beautiful to see all the different modalities of healing you humans work with. In a way, you could say we dolphins always do the same thing. Always, our focus is to bring that which is energetically out of balance into balance. We use our own energy fields to do this. Using sonar is just one of our tools. We also use our evolved feeling capacities, and our consciousness of color, sound and light.

There is one other piece and we almost hesitate to mention it because of our desire to be seen and known by you for who we are and not as a caricature, but we will take the risk. We are very aware of what the soul of a being is going through. All lives are derived from a soul's intent to be here, and to be here for specific purposes. We can sense how things are going for a soul having a human experience. Please hear this lightly. It is a simple and straightforward thing we speak of with this sensing ability we have. Empaths among humans likewise feel these things but do not always know how to keep their inner balance when someone is suffering. They can misconstrue their role as being here to rescue. We do not feel the need to rescue anyone. We do enjoy infusing an atmosphere of lightness where there was heaviness.

In a way, what we do is help create more space for someone to figure out how to help themselves.

So, what of dolphins in captivity in service to humanity in some manner and most expressly doing that which has come to be known as dolphin assisted therapy? Is this something we feel good about? It may sound strange to say, but we don't have an agenda about it. We love humanity and if we are in a position to assist in that way we do best, helping to bring balance, of course we would do that. We deal mostly in our lives with what is, not what should be. Our prime value for ourselves and others is to be free to fully express our incarnate being in a given lifetime. All we do is towards that end. When humans are out of balance and they therefore are not free in the way just described, our presence can be of genuine assistance. When that happens, it is no accident.

the dolphins

LETTER 17

Dear Humans,

Let us talk about weather for a while, and changes that happen on and to the Earth. If you take the long view of the planet's existence and all the extremes it has been through in the 30 plus million years which our species has experienced being here, you can easily see how much happens, and on such a large scale. There have been times in which 90% of animal life on this planet became extinct. There have been ice ages, times when fires raged so extensively that the sun was blotted out for months from the smoke, times when floods erased land masses and mountains exploded up out of the ocean floor. For those of you interested in this topic there is much material for you to explore. It is fascinating to see how much change does take place on this planet, yet life persists. The planet is able to get herself back again, over time.

The concerns many of you have about current climate change is not shared by everyone. Some of you feel it is too late to reverse some of the trends of ice melting at the polar caps and all that will occur as a result. Some of you are fatalistic believing what will be will be and you proceed to live as if everything is the same as always knowing down deep, it is not. Others of you are dedicated to educating and inspiring people to wake up and acknowledge what humans are doing that is contributing to planetary issues and creating havoc. And lastly, many of you live in awareness of the vice grip of the gridlock of opposing perspectives, person to person, group to group and nation to nation, and you wonder how it will be possible to be released into some kind of shared vision and common ground.

You humans are living in the seed bed of the "new" but to you, it is not clear how to get "there" from "here", and what does "there" even look like? City and industrial life is so contrasted to rural and nature infused life and yet, due to your large and growing human population, the two worlds are colliding and the natural world that needs its space and wildness is being encroached upon.

Here is what we have to say about all of the above. The world is changing and yes, humans have contributed to what is happening in nature and with weather. It is also true the planet goes through different stages as well, with humanity or without it. She would still go through ice ages and fires and floods and shifting of land masses. The real issue isn't about the weather per se but is about how you relate to the differences you culturally different humans have, one from the other, and how much you can find the deeper similarities you share.

This planet is so populated that it is getting harder and harder to get away from others who you do not agree with. You are being forced to deal with each other. We suggest there is something about figuring out how to co-operate with others you feel very different from that is getting ready to happen all over this planet in ways you would never have expected. This is another reason we are reaching out to you now, to let you know the changes are trustworthy and that these changes are the keys to opening the doors where you need to enter and live and thrive.

We dolphins deal with alien life forms constantly and about the worst we ever feel the need to do is to ram a shark in the ribs to teach him some manners about looking at us and our young and elderly as prey. We co-operate with the "alien" others, with the shearwater birds with whom we share the spoils when we make a bait ball. We co-operate with human fishermen around the globe by chasing fish to shore for them to net, and then we divide the spoils with their giving back to us our share.

You will discover, and are discovering that in cases of the extremes of weather this planet experiences including the Earth changes she is going through, you need each other and will need each other even more as things progress. When you pull together, there can be explosions of creative and innovative ideas about how to turn threats to well being into shifts of whole new ways of being.

Systems will collapse, ones you would never think could but what the breakdown of resistance you have of coming together to deal with it all will give you is so much more than what will be taken away. We see this clearly.

You have at your disposal the means to destroy yourselves like you have never had before in human history which means, in this transitional period you are in, you are vastly vulnerable to things going awry. Some of the "going awry" has already happened regarding things done to the air and water by pollutants and radiation and the decimation of your oxygen producing and life-rich rain forests.

Even so, there is a beautiful birthing of intent to do better on the parts of ever increasing numbers of people as they become guided by compassion more than any other energy form. Compassion always joins. Out of compassion, things will be assisted to move in the direction of what humans can jointly do. It is too late for blame. Who did what to whom is beside the point because of the degree to which you now see, you are all in the same boat.

The carrying of extreme beliefs is going to be sacrificed because it cannot sustain. How that happens we won't say for it is to be your doing, but we assure you it is the case. That is why we spoke to you before about disempowering beliefs as the gods you have made them. Beliefs can help you get from Point A to Point B, so use them when you need them and then drop them when you do not.

We realize this sounds radical. What we say is not only based on where you are coming from but on where you will be going as a very different human than you have been before. The approach about dropping beliefs is radical, and it is also very balanced if you look at the bigger picture, which we do.

We are suggesting things to you to try on to see how you feel in your whole being, not just in your mind. In the book STRANGER IN A STRANGE LAND, the term "grok" was introduced to suggest knowing something with all of you as we are suggesting here. This word has become part of your lexicon because so many understood the reference. We are asking you to see how much of what we share with you, you can "grok."

There is one last piece we will throw in here about the weather, something that the shamans among you understand very well. Weather is part of all that is, just as you are, so you are linked to weather more than you know. When you humans come together in co-operation and compassion, it effects everything, including weather. The more you explore the power of behaving as one huge pod who have in common that you all are participating in a human experience, the more you will uncover your abilities to have very direct communication with all of nature, including the weather.

This might be a frightening thought, to think you have such powers, but you do have, and it is time for you to claim them. In a way, you simply must, to take care of the next turn on the evolutionary spiral of the whole of humanity. The shackles keeping you from your next level of creative expression are both falling away in spite of you and because of you. You are participating in something unstoppable, and that is the good news.

the dolphins

LETTER 18

Dear Humans,

Something you and we have in common is love of touch and affection expressed through touch. When we dolphins are swimming together and touching, there is something else going on as well. We are very aware of the energy fields of each other and how we are affecting each other on those levels. At the same time, we are aware of the energies in the environment itself and adding one more thing, we are aware of the energy of our whole collective, the pod.

We are able to make all of these adjustments pretty much at once because of how our brains have evolved. Living in the water has given us the luxury of paying more attention to our capacities to experience the manifold expressions of energies within and without. We always are looking to balance out all the variance in the larger field, to align all that vibratory movement in a way that creates harmony. Everything consists of vibration, all thought, feeling, DNA emanations, spiritual sensitivities, everything. It is just one fine orchestration, and we like to conduct.

You humans developing on land over a six times shorter time period than us have likewise evolved your brain and, you have gone a different route than we have. Rather than work with, as your primary focus, your inner awareness of how energy moves within you and how that affects what is outside of you (the external world), you, on the whole, have focused externally on shaping and identifying your environment. At first, these pursuits were about survival needs. Then you expanded to include the desire to explore and figure out what was seemingly outside yourself out of great curiosity and a sense of adventure.

We are aware we are making sweeping generalizations here, but it is to make a point, so bear with us.

You humans have accomplished amazing things, things we are in awe of. However, you have gone so far in your belief that your goal is to control or conquer the world you inhabit that we feel called to step in and share with you our standard of balance in all things that you may observe where course correction is needed.

If you could become as curious and deeply interested in learning what we know of working with natural energies (of which there are many kinds, as you know), you would discover you have the same capacities that we have. No, you do not have sonar abilities just within yourselves, using no instruments or devices. Your approach has been to imitate nature and create devises to help you accomplish what you witness in nature; no small feat. Not to take away from your accomplishments, what we aim to do here is to plant a seed that you are on the brink of awakening some deeper capacities that we have already developed. It is all about recognizing and working with energies from the inside. Here is the thing. You and the energies, no matter what kind or from what level, are all the same stuff. When that really sinks in, a very big light will go off.

Anything that is of you IS you and therefore is something you can work with masterfully eventually. We are not saying this does not involve a process of awakening but when a certain critical mass gets reached on the part of many at the same time, well, you know about that. Things can shift in an eye blink. So much in life is about where you put your focus and that lets you know what will evolve next.

As you let yourself "grok" the ramifications of this letter, it will take you into the place of never again being able to feel about nature that she is "other." She never was, but many of you, in your enthusiasms to grow, forgot that.

We are writing these letters now but we have always been communicating with you in one way or another. When you see us leap in the air while we look you in the eye, we are encouraging you to leap as well. In right time, of course, and knowing when right time is, is an inside job. For so many of you, we suggest you are right in the middle of the time to leap, and leap again, and then leap even more. Don't be afraid or, be afraid if you want to, but either way, exhilaration will follow.

the dolphins

LETTER 19

Dear Humans,

It is such a leap to go from commodity to comrade and companion to equal but that is exactly what you are in the process of doing regarding your relationship with us and in truth with all of nature. Much earlier in your history, animals were to be feared and avoided. Then they became a source of food and clothing and decoration and needed to be trapped and killed. In the case of our cousin the sperm whale, the oil in their head lit whole nations. Horses became mechanisms for fighting wars. Many animals became beasts of burden here to do the heavy lifting, so to speak. Animals in circuses and theme parks and aquariums are used to entertain. Wolves became domesticated and became your dogs and pets along with captured parrots and many other species. And so it has played out.

Now at what we shall call leap time, humans are to shift to calling all of nature brother. Not that many of your "original peoples" did not already do that, but their voices were drowned out by the ambitions of the line of evolution interested in conquering.

The forms "partnering with nature" will take can hardly be imagined yet but we assure you of this: as you allow yourselves to give up the belief that nature is in subservience to the will of humans to create in any way you want . . .when you give that up, something else shows up that will allow you to take your creativity to a whole new level. The visionaries among you can see ahead but for many, this shift takes a giant leap of faith, to let a way of doing and being go that you are convinced you are dependent upon.

In general, large change takes long periods of time and adaptation is eased by things happening incrementally, but every so often, a quantum leap occurs that creates great change of awareness instantaneously. Once the shift occurs, then it is easy to see that it was coming the whole time. Until the shift occurs, it is hard to even imagine it.

You are at a place now where-in you must shift to survive, and most feel this even if they do not talk about it. The fact that planetary resources are not unlimited is one contributing factor but even more to the point is the speed at which this world is becoming a global village which utterly requires transforming how you relate to what you perceive as "other."

We are not speaking to you just about your survival. Our interest is in your thriving. There is a distant song playing and more and more of you are hearing it. Like when you listen to the songs of whales, you are impacted but you don't know why. There is just something about your possible future that you keep sensing in spite of all the breakdown, uproar and dysfunction. The music sneaks up on you. We suggest where this music comes from is your hearing nature in a whole new way.

If you do not yet hear this music, you will, and you will be grateful for it. Your technological advances are actually assisting this process of hearing with new ears for you are connecting with each other globally in real time like never before which allows one person's new perception to rapidly resonate and spread.

A paradox is that this increase in connecting also needs to be balanced with disconnecting from your devices so that you may go deeper into your hearing of nature. Here we are with our refrain again. BALANCE. We always come back to that. That is one of the gifts we have gotten from our long stint on this planet, and it lets us know what awaits you as you enter the next turn of the spiral, for we once were in similar stages of evolution as you are. The forms our growth took were different but the process was the same. Hence, our faith in you.

the dolphins

LETTER 20

Dear Humans,

What a contrast. You made it to the moon with your technology and building abilities. We have built nothing externally, not dams like beavers nor nests like birds. The truth is, we do build and we build extensively, if by build you mean create something where nothing was before.

Our building tools are sound and vibration. For you to appreciate this accomplishment, a gear must be shifted. That gear is that the world of effects (that which you perceive as external using your five physical senses) is no more profound than the realm of cause (vibration). We have no compulsion or inclination towards building externally for we are exceedingly occupied with the intricacies of vibration in its forms of light and sound.

A relatively recent discovery in the quantum physics world is that a vacuum has structure. This is not news to us because we can "see" with sound and hear the structure as geometric forms.

So of what use is this message to you about our capacities? One use is it begins to answer the question of what we are doing with all our brain power. You may wonder, how is what we are sharing here different than reporting an experience someone might report from taking an hallucinogenic substance and having their mind opened to things far outside of what they are used to? It is similar in that you are given an opportunity to go beyond the bounds of your accustomed ways of experiencing life by finding out about what we are up to, and in the case of hallucinogenics, finding out what the intelligence of plant life is up to. In both cases, you are dropping your boundaries so that the world can get bigger and more inclusive. Boundaries also drop with meditative practices and working with advanced masters who understand vibration even more profoundly than we do.

The physical senses of humans are limited to telling you the effects of a very old and somewhat circumscribed story, the story that aligns with how the masses of humans have evolved to this point. Being on Earth so much longer, our species is closer to the memories of the primordial soup we all come from and what allowed us to come into being in the first place. This more intimate connection with our beginnings does not make us better, just older.

You are us and we are you. You don't remember that, and we have never forgotten it. We cannot remind you enough of this connection we have. The competitive strain is so strong in humans because the connections, the continuity of all of life, has been forgotten. So, we remind you, maybe even to the point of irritation at this point.

Having said all this, we are so impressed with what you have managed to create using only a certain segment of what is available to you ultimately. The war and greed part have been a bit jarring but the creativity and courage you have demonstrated over and over we bow to. You have much as a species to feel good about.

It is very important you do not let denied disappointment in yourselves convince you that you have failed. What is off the mark is correctible through the alchemy of love as an energy, a vibration that is far more powerful than its younger sister, sentiment. When we say we love you, we are speaking of the vibration that really is far beyond language. We even hesitate to use the word because it has become misunderstood as being less than it is. But we assure you (and we seem to be doing a lot of that in these letters), if you could see your spirit like we see you, your self-judgment would be absolved immediately as the bigger accuracy replaced it.

Next time you look into the eye of a whale or dolphin, let it register what the eye looking back at you is communicating. It can change many things for you, and expedite a great deal of what your soul wants for you. The intimacy of eye contact with each other, that is, of us with you, is in high service to what is best for both of us. You magnificently give to us as well, when this happens.

the dolphins

LETTER 21

Dear Humans,

You wonder about us and how our being captured and put into captivity affects us. Do we successfully adapt over time once we move past the initial trauma of abduction? There are many who work with dolphins and whales in captivity who become very attached to us. Where there is genuine love, there is always benefit. On our parts, our tendency is to make the best of the situation we find ourselves in.

Our capture is still a case of one group stealing another's freedom. The story of one group oppressing another is as old as time itself, be it human to human, or human to another species. Here is our main point in bringing this topic up. Slavery is no longer tenable, no matter what form it takes. You will increasingly see the evidence of that. This entire planet will amaze you in the manner in which, almost as if nature herself is doing it, there will be a collapse from the inside of anything that robs the freedom of any aspect of nature to express its own spirit.

Change usually occurs incrementally in the march of evolution. Every so often, something a long time coming occurs in the blink of an eye. We suggest that slavery as an institution or an option is on the brink of extinction. It is not just a matter of humans motivated by profit needing to transform their ways and stop robbing us of our freedom to swim with our pod mates on the open seas, or wishing that the ones wishing to protect us be allowed to prevail. This is not about someone being right and someone being wrong and digging into a position. There is something bigger at stake than winning in a tug of war.

In capturing us, you don't just "ruin our day." You put all of humanity in jeopardy because you are taking action on the wrong side of where evolution is going. Our desire is for humanity to cease and desist all slavery so that you do not have to reap the results of adhering to what cannot sustain you.

We are to many people a symbol for freedom as they see us out swimming at sea with wild abandon. Have you ever wondered about the deeper reason we are for you a symbol of freedom? We suggest we remind you of something you once had that you will have again.

Many humans, when they think of freedom, think of being in a position where you can call the shots in your own life. The problem with that way of looking at freedom is that it keeps you in a constant state of fear of losing what you have or having to fight to maintain what is "yours," and to us, there is no freedom in that way of living. You become a slave to your beliefs of what you must do to maintain or to gain.

The reason we do not aspire to that version of freedom is because we live with an awareness of our birth rite just to be who we are innately. It is just how we do life. We have the best of both worlds. We are sanctioned in our own individuality. At the same time, we are cushioned and thrilled by our connection with each other in the pod and the deep roots of belonging that gives us. Our "I" and our "we" are constantly interweaving in the moment.

You humans are ready to learn this dance which in and of itself will transform you into your next stage. We have been nudging you for millennia to watch us and learn this piece of the puzzle. You are so close to making this leap. A word to the wise. Sometimes it is right before the biggest shifts that the biggest resistances kick in. That is one reason some of your shenanigans on this planet that cause the more sensitive ones of you to feel despairing does not cause us to join in that despair. We know better, and we are from the future, remember?

the dolphins

LETTER 22

Dear Humans,

The way you do life, you are very aligned with calendars and dates and clocks and all kinds of grids and time/space locaters. You look at your devices and charts and pages and lists to get your bearings. Working with linear time is a huge part of your orientation to life. You are aware of cycles and things returning as well, such as seasons and phases of the moon, but on the whole, it is the march forward and backward that has you in its throes.

We of the sea are aware of not just linear time but of time as a dimensional experience, more vertical than horizontal for one can dimensionally travel into infinitude, not unlike going up a ladder that never ends. What we are doing differently than you, on the whole, is that we are dimensionally traveling as a means of having life experience while in a physical body. Our bearings are not so much spatial (longitude and latitude) as vibrational. We can vibrate ourselves into different states and thusly have different experiences. We do this using the natural energies of creation, which you also possess. This vibrational awareness has simply not been your focus on your evolutionary path in the way it has been on ours.

Your focus is about building things and learning about the laws of nature in the third dimension where linear time holds sway. In our underwater life of experiencing life as constantly flowing, we have been about the business of seeing what other dimensions have to offer. You experience these other realms as well but mostly do not acknowledge to yourself that you are doing so. The ones who come the closest to exploring in the manner we do are the shamans, the mystics, those interested in the paranormal, and now your physicists are getting on board.

The advantage of refusing to limit yourself to outside designations (clocks, calendars) is that you not only find yourself in a much larger playing field, but in a much less threatening one in that most fear comes from jumping out of the present moment in anticipation of what might be coming. The only way to vertically travel is by staying in this moment.

Another advantage of not getting too married to third dimensionality, where linear time is king, was pointed out by your fine human Albert Einstein when he correctly identified that a problem cannot be resolved on the level it was created. The dimension above always holds the key for the one below.

What we say here will have little meaning for you unless you have first hand experience of what dimensionality is about, and register it consciously. This is another reason we are reaching out to you now. Many of the issues on this planet now in the third dimension are rather dire, yet, solutions await as you allow your vibration to change so that you can visit other dimensions. Shifting to focus on vibrational awareness is not a thinking function. It is a feeling one.

Your minds are meant to be helpful and enjoyable and when you try to get them to be more than that, then you have reached beyond what the limits of the good, the rational and logical can offer you. For the highly intelligent among you, this can be a bitter pill to swallow if you have taken your intelligence to be a measure of your worth.

The gifts by the acknowledged geniuses among you (though we suggest you each have genius of one kind or another) have been astounding throughout your history, part of why we hold you in awe. You could say the gifts were the result of the mind, and we say, yes, but the mind was in service to the heart, even if the donors did not know that. The heart always wants to meet true need. However the wheel came to be, it was a gift of need meeting, and therefore of love. You are far more awash in love than you perhaps have considered yourselves to be. We say this not in chastisement, but in just offering perhaps a change in perspective.

the dolphins

LETTER 23

Dear Humans,

We wish to write here about the enrichment that can come from our two species opening up to a more pronounced "cultural exchange," as it were. We do share with each other in bits and pieces but that sharing has not become integrated into our overall cultures as two species.

This is a time on the planet for the diversity of cultures to open to each other like never before, human to human, but also human to our species as well as to other species. In order for this exchange to occur on a large scale, prejudice must be dealt with. Prejudice always comes from fear of "other" and simple lack of understanding and familiarity.

You humans have the means of dissolving so many boundaries even as you sometimes become entrenched in strongly held beliefs or viewpoints. Right under those seemingly bedrock beliefs is a fast running river of openness and flexibility built on self-trust. It is our impression that it is hard for you to reach this level of openness and desire to explore "other" because self-trust is a bit of a weak note in your musical scale.

You are not used to letting your sensitivity to vibration (detecting in your feeling nature) be your main source of guidance. We suggest you use this guidance more than you know. If asked, you would probably conclude that you use your mind to decide what to do, what to believe, and what is worth valuing. Your mind is where prejudice can get a toe hold so, limits are in place that can hold you back if this is what you most rely upon.

Let us give you some examples of how you use our guidance system more than you know. You are drawn to music whose vibration works best with your own field. Same is true regarding your response to color, and shape. Many times when you are enjoying listening to someone speak, it is not the words or messages that you are primarily having a positive response to. It is the vibration of their voice, and of their auric field coming through their voice. Appreciating the message is more the icing on the cake.

One reason certain people are considered to be charismatic is because they have discovered how to let the truth of who they are on all of their vibrational levels come out fully to be shared with others as a gift given. The mode of sharing is not as important as the fact that they are not holding back their essence.

If you try to elicit just from words what feels right to you, you will minimally get confused and maximally, will get in situations where you feel betrayed and led down a primrose path. That is what we perceive as to how you reduce your self- trust. The irony is, the less self-trust, the more rigid the clinging to a belief.

Well you know you are living in a fast changing and somewhat upside down world. The more you are with us, the more you will be able, almost by osmosis, to stay in the present moment and trust your natural attractions while by-passing previously held prejudices.

To allow oneself to flow very spontaneously from moment to moment trusting the feelings of attraction can be very scary in the beginning. There is a fear of making a mistake. That fear primarily comes from lack of practice and also from cultural conditioning. We do not desire to talk you into or out of anything but rather to just point in certain directions and then you can just let things shake out on their own, which they will at any rate. We are of the mind that you stand to gain by getting more keys to freedom sooner, so we speak up. Learning to trust the information that comes to you from your feeling nature will ultimately add ever so much exhilaration to your life, especially as you move past the fear of being wrong or doing something wrong.

How can our two species come together more powerfully and influentially than we have before? What would that look like? We see this coming together already beginning to happen and it seems to be, we almost want to say, trying to happen, like an idea whose time has come. The lightening fast ability now that humans have for communicating in real time globally is expediting the sharing of encounters with us which are never, we assure you, accidental. You humans are riding a wave. We are not creating this wave but we are getting on it and slightly in front so that we can turn around to let you know that our connecting with each other is happening. There is nothing we need to fabricate to bring it about. It is happening on its own. That being the case, why do we need to say anything? To confirm what might be just enough under your conscious awareness to be lost on you without a tap on the shoulder.

These times are so pregnant with opportunities for rewards and enhancements. We are no longer content to sit and watch the show. We have waited a long time for this period of unfoldment. Now that we are here, we speak up to see how many of you can hear what we share. We also are excited beyond measure about what we stand to gain from you as you make your leap. There is much that we will create together that we do not know about, but we feel it coming. The vibration is already here.

the dolphins

LETTER 24

Dear Human,

The content of this letter is a bit complex. We will do our best to make it clear and as concise as possible. We include it because it provides another major key to freedom which we are all about sharing with you. As a species, there is an ability we carry having to do with the link between the present moment and the faculty and function of memory.

In general, members of the animal kingdom are considered to operate in the present without accessing the past or anticipating the future. They are considered to have the rudiments of memory. A dog recognizes a trusted owner (though we wince a bit using the word "owner"). What we mean here by "memory" is the ability to dwell in the past in a state of linear recall. It is assumed animals do not do that. Even animals mourning a lost loved one are assumed to be sad without really knowing why, just sensing something is wrong or missing. (Where these assumptions come from is a mystery to us.)

What we wish to do here is introduce you to something dolphins and whales do that is something you can also do, though most of you do not, at least not extensively. It is possible to access the layers of feeling of the past or of the future into the present moment to operate in the present according to the greater designs of your soul and spirit. You do not need to have the particulars of memory in the form of linear recall, but only the feeling tones, the meaning stored within, in order to do this.

The more conscious you are of the designs of your soul and spirit, the better, for that is how you know what, in the moment, is yours, and what you can allow to just pass by. An example of what we mean here by saying designs of your soul and spirit would be those flashes you have when you feel fully aware of who you are and why you are here and you automatically fully engage. You may never find words for what we speak of here, but you can recognize what we mean.

Memories are valuable, whether they be of the past or of the future (and yes, future memories do exist) for it is the texture found within the memories that creates the richness of a life lived.

Even those humans who feel they are losing their memory function are still able to have the ability to pull meaning from memory into their present moment. There is an account of your ex-President Reagan who was in an advanced stage of Alzheimer's who pulled a small copy of the White House out of a gold fish bowl because he could feel its significance in his life, even though his linear recall was gone. The molecules in you that were part of the Big Bang can communicate meaning to you in the present moment in ways you can feel and utilize (again, for your soul's purpose) even though you cannot name them.

How is any of this useful to you? We are offering you here a hint of what the kind of freedom of which we are a living representative is all about. As your great man Gautama Buddha showed you, suffering comes from attachments. Memory, as a reaching into and lingering in the past (which can be very pleasant as a pastime for many humans) can be a way of clinging so as not to suffer loss. What we are stressing here is that even if you never again visit the past in that manner, the past is not really gone. It is in you and of you and will re-appear in the present as a feeling you may not be able to source, but your soul can receive what it needs from the essence of the memory. Even if they are unpleasant or traumatic memories that are being utilized in the present in this manner, it is to meet the design of your soul. These "sneak attacks" are behind many moods that come upon you out of nowhere that you cannot source. We lightly call them "attacks" for in truth, they are in service to your enrichment. All feelings combine to give the ground for growth.

One reason we do not judge what humans do to us out of not being more awakened to who we really are (both in general and in connection to you) is that our consciousness has learned to use everything that happens for the enriching of our growth in time present. We do not impose thoughts of what should be. We work with what is and hold to our soul designs which have so much to do with going deeper into what inner freedom is, and exploring the heights and depths of consciousness. Living this way takes fear out of the equation which is a huge element of being able to be inwardly free.

For you humans, fear is an ever present companion to the degree that you think ahead and live in the future in your minds. You cannot feel fear in the present. The sages have shared this wisdom throughout the ages and still, you yield to the temptation to jump ahead, and your neurology follows close behind.

We would like to make a distinction here. All physical bodies desire to live, therefore your body will feel strong responses to a threat on its existence even as your spirit feels no such threat. When a body becomes hyper-alert in response to threat, that is not what we are referring to as fearing something in the future. Perhaps, a gazelle running from a lion is feeling a sense of dread, something impending, but as soon as the lion takes the gazelle down, a surrender happens that is not as mentally painful as most humans think, for the gazelle is not associating its experience with an idea of being a victim. Like most animals, it is in the moment and going with the flow being aware of what is going on. We suggest it is as much the lion as it is itself in such moments for, to animals, the fact of all of nature being connected is not a thought. It is cellular truth. In the animal world, the present moment beautifully allows peaceful co-operation with what is happening as part of something bigger.

Anything you have ever experienced is part of everything you will ever experience so you cannot be separated from what you are creating. Everything, including the end of your body and unpleasantness attached to that end are just condiments to the bigger dish.

We do not wish for this to turn into a philosophical lecture. You have heard many renditions of what we are saying here. We wanted to give you our version because it is coming from those (us) who constantly access the past and the future but only as they belong in the present, where fear cannot dwell. Living this way now is like breathing for us (and the way we breathe corresponds to the message we relay here, which we explain in another letter). We have not always known how to live this way but used our complex brains to figure it out. Scientists scratch their heads at what we are doing with our complex brains since we are not building anything externally. We would say, we are building highways in our consciousness, without the distractions of doing all that you do. Though we don't go in the direction you go, we have to admit, what you have built is impressive. We give you that and now, there is a balance problem that must be addressed.

The end of fear is on its way on this planet as part of the leap humanity will take. You can keep caution and awareness of danger but fear is ready to be evolved out of you once enough of you learn how to let it go and create a critical mass. Life beyond fear is limitless in its creative potential. This is what you have to look forward to, and no, you will not be bored with unhealthy fear out of the picture.

the dolphins

LETTER 25

Dear Humans,

As useful as categorizing can be, letting something remain nameless a little longer keeps the door open to accessing more experience. What your scientists have accomplished via looking for patterns and closely tracking what can be perceived, correlated and measured through the five senses is mind boggling. Somewhere in human history, it was decided if you could name something, you could control it. Now (though as we introduce this to you, it can sound threatening) there is a new game in town. It is about a shift in which you let go of the need to control and open to the desire to experience without prematurely labeling what is being experienced.

Many of you are finding yourselves experiencing your familiar world in unfamiliar ways. You feel exhilarated, enticed, confused and disoriented. Some have described it as feeling as if two worlds are colliding. What you are accustomed to feels momentarily unfamiliar. What is unfamiliar somehow reminds you of something you once understood but have forgotten.

Who has these experiences? The answer is . . . everyone, but many of you quickly override these "felt" experiences and use your mind to respond to your identity of what you think you are supposed to be paying attention to.

This "bleed through" kind of experience will be happening more and more. What frequently accompanies these kinds of awareness's is a sense of familiar boundaries dissolving. During these times, it is important that you rely on a profound sense of self-knowing and intimacy with who you are at core. You need to go deeper than identifying with the body you are in, the family you were born into and the beliefs of your culture. This depth of self knowing can be hard come by for it can run counter to some of the perspectives you grew up with held by the ones you love and who cared for you. We assure you, this pearl of great price, this self knowledge, is your greatest protection as you go through some large leaps of the evolution of your very species.

As you learn the truth of your being apart from anything outside of you, a paradox is that this will allow you to align with others who are likewise deeply self aware. Once this happens, prejudice will fall away and you will have with each other a virtual dolphin pod.

Through our lengthy evolution, we dolphins have found the pivot point in which we get to be completely fleshed out in our individuality, and at the same time, very fluidly connected to a pod of family and friends. Only by being free of fear of loss of external identity can you live on the tip of this pivot point. We would say, this is not where two worlds collide, but where they coalesce.

In the beginning, attempting to establish this fine balance can feel like being torn by opposites .Evolutionarily speaking, it can take millennia going back and forth between valuing the individual and membership in the group, sometimes called a tribe. And then there comes the time of the merge. That is where we see you humans as being on the brink, and is a huge part of the leap you are making.

Since we dolphins are already living this way, being around us or, as we prefer to say since it brings up our favorite topic of "vibration," when you are in our field, you can be assisted to let go in trust to living in a way where you can create without fear. Many fears and layers of fears are leaving the planet at this time. You are not there yet but what we describe is the direction you are headed.

We are here to help you trust what, as of yet, has no name other than perhaps to call it "freedom." That comes the closest. And just so you know, you can join us and be in our field in consciousness as easily as in our physical presence. All you have to do is feel us as a vibration.

the dolphins

LETTER 26

Dear Humans,

We would like to share with you something of the Dolphin Body Politic. When you take the functioning whole of us, you get something very kaleidoscopic in nature and expression. Since we do not have institutions that we lock into and feel allegiance to, we are free to adapt to the needs and desires of the moment in ways that are very fluid and artful. We have learned this way of being by living in the water where flowing is a constant. On the surface of the water, there can be a dead calm, but under the seas and rivers is all about movement and currents.

Our evolutionary impetus by living in the water has been equally focused on our body's shape and functions as well as on the development of our cognitive abilities. If we were judged by human standards, we would probably be identified as being hyperactive because being still is not something we do naturally.

You humans by dwelling so much on ways to take care of your needs and survival on land with its strong gravitational field have developed ways to live so entirely in your mental processes that you can almost, for long periods of time, forget you have a body. Your world becomes whatever your mind is thinking about, and "balance," one of our central tenets for living, becomes misaligned.

You are body and mind and spirit and to have and maintain balance, movement in the body is necessary. For you deep meditators who can be perfectly still for minutes and hours and even days on end, this is a different matter. In these cases, much like when you are sleeping or even including passing from this life, you are realm jumping and visiting aspects of consciousness well outside the sphere of what most in the human condition are paying attention to. You are drinking from the well of the Eternal which is a whole other topic.

Dolphins do not meditate separately from the rest of our activities. Our lives are a living meditation because of our degree of openness to whatever we allow to weave into our present moment from any contributing realm. We do not experience our bodies so much as being matter as we do of it being energy.

For humans, meditating is like escaping the heaviness of gravity. Dolphins only feel heavy if they find themselves out of water for a period of time. We find that experience extremely difficult to endure. When you see beached whales and dolphins, we are undergoing something that you cannot relate to even if you lay on the ground next to us. We say this not to make you feel sorry for us but to help you understand the very real differences between you and us as we share this planet. We once were land mammals and we returned to the water (which all life came from originally) and we have never looked back. The reason for that choice on our part is speculated as having been to follow a food source. That was part of the reason but once in the water, our evolution shaped itself very differently than it would have been had we stayed on land, and we are glad for it.

We are not suggesting humans should all begin the long, slow climb to becoming amphibious (though "the aquatic ape theory" suggests that has already happened). We are not looking to change your considerable progress as land mammals. Our main point in these letters is to let you know we wish to pool our resources and conjoin the best of what the intelligence in the seas and the intelligence on the land have brought forward in our parallel evolutions.

We share our differences so you can see what is there for you to benefit from knowing about. We are very eager to learn more from you. We may be quite a bit older than you (around 25 million years) but you have done things and developed capacities we know little of and are intrigued by, especially space travel. For those who idealize us and ascribe superiority to us as a species over the human race, we do not feel superior. We feel love and admiration for you, even seeing the ways you are out of balance and off course in your current trajectory. We trust you to course correct, and if anything in these letters can serve to inspire you to do that, nothing would please us more, just so you know. We aspire for your fulfillment.

the dolphins

LETTER 27

Dear Humans,

One thing we are doing quite on purpose in communicating with you through these letters is de-emphasizing vernacular when talking about complex subject matter. For the more scientific among you, anything too vague and etheric sounding can be off-putting. For the consciousness cosmonauts, conclusions can be too easily jumped to. Our desire is to take you more deeply into the rich waters of your feeling field and give you a chance to grow more confident in experiencing without having to name anything prematurely which can result in putting the brakes on what your neurology is now capable of giving to you.

Since human language is word based using concrete symbols, the idea of moving beyond this terrain to advance your consciousness can feel threatening, yet this is what we are encouraging you to explore. We suggest that many decisions and conclusions on your part are more feeling based than you acknowledge to yourselves. Yet, the human tendency in the highly intellectualized place you are on in your evolutionary path can veer towards shutting down to the "beyond words wisdom" that lives within the huge range of your feeling states.

Feelings include, but are more than emotions. Feelings are like colors or tones or even subtle scents that have the power both to inform and to motivate. Artists are very connected to these realms. Writers, even though using a verbal medium, will report how the writing just happens, comes from their muse as they respond to an inner directive that is not verbal, but is felt. There is much music in words - cadence and rhythm and tonality. Writing is so much more than bare boned meaning. Poets understand this.

If you think we are suggesting that every human is an artist, we are. You are at a point in your evolution in which solutions to global problems are begging to be freed creatively without being restricted by what has come before. Creating collectively and individually (that pivot point we mentioned) is available in a way now that should not be over-thought but rather entered into as a grand adventure.

We continue dropping hints to you as we initially said we would be doing. We speak of what we understand from first hand experience. We are not saying we do or do not have words and language. We prefer to make you curious about another realm of communicating we heavily rely upon that is greater in its application than the use of discreet symbols.

At this point, let us bring up our use of sonar. There can be no deceit among us because we can literally see right through each other. Emotions always have physical correspondents so we easily know what each other is emotionally experiencing at any given moment. This is where a large amount of our freedom comes from. You have no idea how much energy and life force gets used up when you humans hide from each other in ways both subtle and convoluted.

There is a way in which humans enjoy their secrets. We are the opposite. We enjoy utter openness. Our evolutionary paths have played a role in the creating of these differences between you and us. More on this later.

We do need to warn you about something. The more you are around us, the more our influence will begin to rub off on you. As that happens, we suggest you will be happier. All beings are happier when they are more free to live in trust and relaxation that it is safe to be open about who they are.

We will save for our next letter how you rub off on us, and why we seek that.

the dolphins

LETTER 28

Dear Humans,

So now we will share how you rub off on us. Proximity to you, whether from in the water or from a boat is something that is meaningful to us, more than you might imagine. The reason for that is the more we connect with you, the more we can feel the Earth herself assisted, for our interaction forms "a third thing" so to speak. This third thing is needed at this time for it is made up of a vibration that raises up everything around it.

You may wonder, if this is so, what happens when humans hunt us, harm us, capture us and even kill us. We are in proximity, so where is "the third thing" in these cases? We still hold out for it for as we have said before, we never give up on you. We will keep asking you to dance until you finally and conclusively say yes.

We are happy to report that more and more of you are feeling our invitation to connect and responding with a resounding "YES!" We can read what is going on with you when you are in the water with us or even just looking at us from a boat. We see what is in your eyes and we feel what you carry in the field around your body. Yes, it is true sometimes we ignore you when we are involved in the complexities of the interactions within our pod. Also, we are very sensitive to intention and if, for example, your desire to be close to us is not a match for who we are in the moment, we will not acknowledge you. To us, social interactions are based on the blending of vibrations, not on rules of etiquette or manners.

You humans, as we have alluded to, like to stay partially hidden. You like to get close to each other but not too close until you decide vulnerability is emotionally safe or desirable. You sometimes use "manners" to manage these considerations. To you, this is a way of not rushing into too much openness before you are ready.

This observation on our part is not meant as a criticism, for only you know if this way of relating to each other is worthwhile. We suspect that the habits of staying partially hidden from each other is such a pervasive way you have of doing things that you do not give much credence to the alternative way of being completely open and transparent. These "artful dodgings" have deep roots within your psyches so would not likely change overnight, even if you decide you want that. However, the more our evolutionary paths co-mingle, the more many "third things" are going to show up that will allow breathtaking shifts to occur much faster than you would have thought possible.

Change does not have to be planned and sought out in the traditional ways of plotting steps towards a desired goal. Goals are fine and for you humans, can be highly motivating. We dolphins work more with taking all elements and vibrations and creating anew in the moment knowing that we always go for balance and we are willing to be surprised with what we create "out of the nowhere into the here." The seeking of balance, from moment to moment, is our golden key, and the way we detect balance is by the harmony experienced within our feeling states.

When you humans expand your feeling states, we get very excited for that lets us know many new "third things" are at hand and ready to manifest, and that Gaia, our shared planet, will benefit. We, being from the future, have seen what possible futures are coming this way so we already know something of what our ultimate collaboration will allow to manifest. We dare not say too much for you would believe some of what we hint at is too good to be true. Because of the timing of the turning of the spiral of evolution of the whole Earth, the visions we glimpse are not too good. They are appropriately good as an outcome to our long journeys. To get to the place of these future visions, we have, you and us, much to do, together. It can be a delightful doing or a harsh doing. We vote for delightful.

the dolphins

LETTER 29

Dear Humans,

There is a movement that began in Finland in 2010 declaring dolphins and whales non-human persons with all the rights there-in. India in 2013 became the first nation to make creating a "dolphinaria" illegal since dolphins have been agreed upon to be persons in that nation. This is a tremendously significant shift for a number of different reasons.

What we have here is a different world view in which other species have the same inalienable rights as humans. For some of you, this is a big stretch and you find it hard to accept at the outset because of how long the planetary citizenship of animals has not been a serious consideration.

Coinciding with this new movement for our kind is a corresponding opening up on the part of the scientific community of awareness of the much greater similarities in human and animal consciousness than ever before believed. The evidence is mounting on this point.

These trends bode well for humans from an evolutionary standpoint and, for some of you, it induces fear about re-thinking so many aspects of your relationship with the animal kingdom (remembering that you humans also have an animal nature which you tend to be wary of). Even re-thinking basic things like your diets comes into play as you allow the implications of a new way of regarding the animal world to sink in.

Re-thinking all of this will be necessary and is important and, can be intimidating. We would like to throw in a suggestion that you not worry so much about the new ways of holding things in your mind, but go into the deep end of the pool. Let yourself be guided by what lives deep inside your own nature which maybe you do not visit often enough. We know we may sound a bit like a broken record but we did warn you in some earlier letters we would be repeating ourselves. Your best guidance and greatest creativity comes from these levels so when you are looking to make a large shift in awareness, you could not find a better place to be situated, than in the rich and colorful realm of the feelings.

There is so much polarity right now amongst you humans based on varying beliefs that are being tenaciously adhered to. Giving up the need to be right is a daunting proposition to many of you. In the realm of feelings, there is no "right." There is just appropriateness to what the life in you is drawn to create in a state of trust and relaxation. In that place, you do not have to fear someone with a different viewpoint. That is where we come in.

By being around us actually or in your imagination, you can go deeper and deeper, like sinking into the sea, into your rich and rewarding feeling states. This is one of the ways we rub off on you. We help you open up a space where the new can gain admittance. As to how we do that, it is the same way we do everything, by interacting with other fields using our own familiarity with all manner of energy to assist the process. You pick up what we know so quickly when you do spend time with us. We have seen it so many times.

We are so heartened by choices we see you increasingly leaning into. Even in some of your what could be called destructive choices, we still respect you for we understand you can only do what you are ready for.

Massive change and the need for it does occur in the evolution of humanity and for the planet herself. When the evolutionary force pushes forward and is resisted, the results can be hard going. This force cannot be resisted indefinitely and we would suggest this is a time when it cannot be resisted at all. Free will is written in the fine print of human experience so you get to call the shots about many things. If you choose to use this period of evolution to shift from a thought based model to a feeling based model, the story line will unfold differently. Your brilliance of intellect can turn into wonderful helpmates in service of establishing what we like to call "the third thing." Your mind is a beautiful tool. We are not suggesting otherwise. It is just no longer the way through to more ease and freedom. It needs to follow, not lead.

Since these letters are cognitive instruments, our message to you can seem contradictory. Some of what we say will fall into place more easily down the road. For now, we will use what we have in the way of explaining just to get us to the next place.

Thank you for hanging in with us as we cross the great divide between us. This divide is becoming smaller almost by the moment. Another reason for reaching out to you now, is you can hear us better than you have been able to before. We are taking advantage, hopefully in the best of ways.

the dolphins

LETTER 30

Dear Humans,

We dolphins have been communicating with you humans for so many centuries but the way we have been doing it has not gotten your attention to any great degree except in a time of pre-recorded history which you do not have any record of. The exception, throughout our time together has been the ones of you who have been able to slow your vibration down enough to hear the wind and water speak to you, and to hear us.

In your eagerness to move forward, you have concentrated your brain waves in a certain spectrum that has allowed you to feel you could push your advantage in dealing with what you perceive as being the external world. There have always been those among you who have sought the inner worlds of Spirit but as a young race of beings, relatively speaking, you have chosen to focus on what could be studied and measured to then help you establish your library of what you considered to be facts. Your factual knowledge kept upgrading itself and you have been fine with that so long as you were content with how the upgrades were determined.

To your credit, you covered much ground within the confines of the parts of your being you were working with. One thing you did do, that we find a bit confounding, is that you handed over your relationship with Spirit to others to interpret and then, in turn, you would answer to these others. Masters of Spirit have walked on your planet and shared their Light and you then would answer to them, which they never asked of you nor wanted.

We dolphins have kept our relationship to Spirit, which we recognize as the source of our being, as integral to daily life as breathing. Interestingly, breath is spirit, so this is more than a metaphor.

As mentioned before, we choose every breath we take which could, evolutionarily speaking, seem like risky business. As a highly emotional species, which we are in, in the instances of not having learned how to master the rambunctious part of our nature (our emotions), we could just decide to stop breathing in a fit of temper or despair. Even as a human child sometimes will hold its breath to get its way, that rebellious act only lasts so long before automatic breathing kicks in. For a dolphin, the breath holding could easily become fatal. Maturing emotionally is something we pretty much had to learn.

We have learned, in our long journey on Earth, much about working successfully with our emotions. Given the tremendous stress it causes us to be abducted from our pods and kept in captivity and made to become very different beings than we were meant to be, the number of incidents of dolphins and whales acting out towards humans hardly exists. You have no idea the number of centuries this level of emotional management required to develop. That is one reason we are patient with the way humans are led around by their emotions. We have been there, but we digress.

Our initial topic for this letter is about how we communicate with you. A primary way is through your subconscious. We show up in your dreams. We become the subject matter of great literature (MOBY DICK). Artists paint and sculpt us. These things are no accident.

Now, though, we feel the need to be more direct and to come out of the watery closet, so to speak. We wish to communicate with you and connect with you by intermingling our fields in such a way that you associate us with certain feeling states. As you find yourselves caught up in the drama of life on this planet at this pivotal time, your mind is going to go on binges of trying to sort things out. The sheer intensity of your mental processes drives you to need to escape into entertainment and distraction to cut yourselves some slack. We are swimming into your life to help you discover a whole other and under-considered field of options . . . your profound feeling nature. We are aware of our redundancy in our messages to you but repetition in a world filled with distractions becomes something of a necessary evil.

You are so close to becoming free in a whole new way but you are also in the most vulnerable stage of re-birth where things could go awry. We say this not to put fear in you but rather to put awareness in you at the very time when the good that awaits you can be accessed more easily than ever before. You are absolutely the ones that will make the good possible. Without your co-operation, the shifts that want to occur on this planet cannot happen.

We happen to know what you will choose which would indicate the outcome is assured. Paradoxically, in your linear time realm, you still are going to have to choose and act according to the degree of Light you carry. The privilege of your being in a body in such transforming times may not be something you are constantly aware of but once you have shifted enough, you will count as more precious than gold that you got to participate.

the dolphins

LETTER 31

Dear Humans,

Let us speak to you for the moment about SOUND. It is a word that we are connected to in every sense. We see with sound using echolocation. Pod consciousness is of sound mind and, more importantly, of sound heart for we understand, as the first nations' people have expressed, that thinking with the heart is THE WAY to proceed on our shared planet. They understand, as do we, that although our minds differ, individual to individual, our hearts share the same cadence. Lastly, and we love this piece, when a dolphin or whale is diving deep, it is called "sounding." That is not an accidental metaphor.

As we have indicated, we experience life in the vertical (time present) going up and down through the planes and dimensions. Linear time (horizontal) is not our main line of travel. We "sound" both up and down.

When the large whales sound the depths of the sea, that is not just a physiological feat. They are going into the depths of the feeling state (of which water is a representative) of nature herself, or Gaia, whichever you prefer.

Feelings are more than just emotion. Feelings entail vast realms of awareness and sensitivities. Whales in the depths of our oceans are in service to the balance and evolution of our planet. If you humans lose them, you will most assuredly lose your overall ability to chart your course forward to this next large stage of your evolution. It is at least important that you hear about what the whales are doing for "the whole" whether you understand it or not.

WE are not speaking here of sentimental love for a species. We are alerting you to a very important part of the business of keeping balance while in the middle of change and how the whales are assisting. The movie STAR TREK IV was more accurate than anyone knew when it came out in 1986, for those of you who remember it. Our letters to you would be incomplete without planting this seed.

the dolphins

LETTER 32

Dear Humans,

We have spoken to you of death. We will make this last letter (for now) about that book-end to death called birth. When dolphins are born, as we shared in another letter, we are surrounded by a field of love, welcoming and ease that has the effect of launching the new life into the vibration of joy from day one.

Human birthing is extremely varied in how it is viewed and undertaken, especially when you consider all the different cultural and environmental aspects over millions of years.

Here we are now, you and us, in the 21st century with humanity being on the brink of whole new ways of doing and being. We saved bringing up the topic of human birth for the last on purpose. How a child comes into this world is the single most formative thing that happens to that embodied soul. There are cases of traumatic births in which the soul goes on to live a remarkable life. We are not speaking of birth circumstances as dooming anyone. Still, know this. A child coming into this world housing his or her great spirit in a small helpless body needs all the love and support he or she can get. Nothing springboards a newborn into a trust of life more than a felicitous birth reception, and nothing that follows can completely make up for the lack of being received with great celebration and recognition of the one coming in.

For humans, what contributes to such an idyllic birth experience? This is for you to discover and many are already doing just that. The dots are being connected. Here is some of what you are coming up with: the gifts of water births; the assisting of women to remember to go deep within, while birthing, into a state of trust of their cellular memory so they can discover resources they did not know they had; the use of quiet, sounds of nature, soft music, low lights, flower scents and essential oils; the presence of friends and family; and whenever possible, being in nature. You are discovering so many avenues worthy of exploring with your deep feeling nature. It is in those depths that you will find a richness of memory of what can assist you in your present moment whether that be in the middle of a contraction or just trying to attune to what feels right to you as the time of birth nears. We are well pleased with your new considerations around birthing.

This topic would not be complete if we failed to mention what some of you are attracted to that you call dolphin assisted water births. This is, among your species, a controversial idea. What we have to say about this idea is that, like all ideas that feel radical to the masses, it has to find its rightful place and expression. For a fact, our love of humanity in combination with our mastery of working with energy fields to find what you might call the Golden Mean i.e. that place of optimal balance, makes us a good ally for you in any endeavor. You change when you spend time with us so a woman in labor would feel a very different experience of what she is going through with our presence. For one, we can entrain your vibration to one of more ease and balance using our own energy field and/or even using sonar.

We are not saying you should have us physically present when you are giving birth so much as we are encouraging you to trust in your own opening awareness of what feels right for you. You are all like flowers opening, spreading your petals with the help of the sun and the rain. We wish to be your sun and rain as you evolve into a much more expanded understanding of how powerful an entrance to this world is for a soul. Think of us. Listen to our sounds. Watch us in person or on film, from on the water or in the water. All doorways of birth, whether through your body or that of another, will benefit as a result of your letting yourself be carried by the waves of your consciousness as it says "yes" to its expansion.

Our relationship with you is meant to become closer now in ways that will be showing up in some surprising forms. Why would childbirth not be part of that closeness? We do not have specific agendas with you other than wanting to connect and share and ultimately partner in giving love back to this planet in the ways we choose to live on her. Freedom is central to our view of the privilege of being alive so we say to you, do what you will. If you can appreciate that we love your species, no matter what, we will be gratified that you figured that out, or believed us when we told you, whichever came first.

the dolphins

LETTER 33

Dear Humans,

You have now read our letters and can put the book down and go on with your lives. We are so pleased to have been able to open to you in this manner. Every letter contains so much love for you that it is hard to put into words. The love comes from our being able to see you so clearly as souls in a body.

If you take nothing else away from what we have shared, please take with you both our love and admiration for your species. Some of you feel embarrassed, indicting yourself for imagining you are so slow to evolve. You have come further than you know. The parts of your world that are so hurting and so bruised and misaligned are not going to stay that way, and you are the ones that will see to it. Even the most stubborn and resistant of you are going to find "the third thing." You don't have to take our word for it. The truth will out.

Yes, you could make the next turn of the evolutionary spiral more difficult than it has to be, and you may choose to do that, but the turn of the spiral will happen. We are part of how that plays out too but in partnership with you. We are stuck with each other, you might say.

We extend ourselves to you here and now in what we hope is the best of ways. So much awaits. One thing is certain. Your and our fates are meshed together so, let's get on with it. Shall we?

Expect us to start showing up more and more in your awareness. Everything, including our beachings, is a communication. Don't be surprised at anything about human and dolphin encounters. This is the age of the improbable.

one last signing off, for now, the dolphins

About the Author

Cover Photo by Jim Abernathy

Muriel Lindsay lives on a barrier island off the coast of Georgia having moved there 15 years ago for the specific purpose of connecting with the dolphins who live in the surrounding waters.. She moved there to find a way to answer to an inner knowing she has carried her whole life. The knowing is that there is something she is supposed to come to understand and then share about the human/dolphin/whale connection. In that spirit of investigation, she has spent 15 years doing what she calls "participatory research" which basically amounts to just hanging out with dolphins on their terms, in the wild, both in and on the water, while opening all of her mental, emotional, physical and spiritual channels.

She has been taught by dolphins in ways that nothing else in life has conveyed quite so powerfully and she knew it was important that many humans would come to receive this benefit whether they were around dolphins in the flesh or not. To her, this connection, human to dolphin and/or whale, is ancient, significant and in need of being brought to light at this time on a fast changing planet.

In 2007, she published "The Chronicles of the Savannah River Dolphins" sharing about five years of experiences with her "teachers" and friends, the dolphins.

Prior to moving to her current home on Tybee Island Muriel was a teacher/healer who traveled the world to gather knowledge from many ancient grounds that would assist her with what she is currently doing. She is one of those who knows that something very large is wanting to be birthed on this jewel of a planet we share.

Muriel is single but never alone. Married to Nature, one might say. Her household includes one Border Collie/Husky mix (way too smart for his own good), a full Husky, a Maine Coon cat and a second cat, a leopard in a tabby cat's body.

For more information, go to: www.muriellindsay.com

Book Club Guidelines for
THE DOLPHIN LETTERS

1) What do you consider to be the central idea or premise of the book? Do you agree with the author that the information in these letters is vital to the welfare of the human race at this particular time in human history? If so, why?

2) Does the concept of collaborating with another species in a very conscious and deliberate way feel like something you are prepared to consider? Does doing that require a humbling of humans' self image as being the dominant species on the planet? Does this offend anyone's religious sensibilities?

3) How does the information shared in these letters affect your daily lives full of personal demands? Does reading the letters support your ability to deal with the complexities of your lives? How?

4) What do you make of how the author came to receive these letters? Is it even important to understand that? Is it enough to just register how you are affected, both in your body and in your feeling nature when you read the letters?

5) Do you notice anything when you re-read the letters? Do you feel that in re-reading them like you are reading them for the first time? If so, what do you make of that?

6) What are the implications in these letters for the future? of humanity? of the planet? Do you feel more encouraged about things you were previously discouraged about? If you do, why do you think that is?

7) Are solutions offered to crucial issues, either personal or planetary? Are hints given by the dolphins inspiring to you or do

you feel frustrated that you still have so much to figure out? What specific comments or passages did you find stimulated your creativity about how to deal with issues (on any level)?

8) What most surprised you in the letters? What most empowered the sense of a difference you could personally make? What did you find you had to keep re-reading to understand? What did you find you were the most interested in discussing with someone else to help work out your own creative inclinations?

9) Did the letters wake up in you some kind of call to action? Was there anything in the letters that alerted you in some new fashion to an arena where you are very attracted to making a difference? If so, what?

10) Do you agree that humans ARE Nature, as opposed to being separate from her? Have you always felt that way? Does this change your priorities from those that do not share this perspective? How? Do the letters give you guidelines about how to take steps to turn things around regarding the resources on our planet? How does the idea of collaborating with the intelligence in the waters in a new way (not yet revealed) affect you? Do you have any inspirations about what forms that might take?

11) Does reading the letters embolden you to be willing to "play more outside the box?" If so, in what way?

12) Is it hard to accept the notion of being taught by another species? What gets stirred up in you when you let that possibility sink in?

13) What do you notice about the tone of the letters that affects how you read and absorb them? How would you describe this tone?

14) Which of the letters did you respond to the most vulnerably? What in the letters seems to hold a key for you as to how to become safer, more free to be who you are at depth and more excited about the future? This question is where the rubber meets the road for you the individual reader, and is where sharing with the whole group will most energize the group itself and allow something similar to what the dolphins refer to as "pod consciousness" to occur.

15) What was your main take away after reading all 33 letters for the first time? What changed in re-reading them? In reading them a third time, what changed yet again?

16) How, during period of studying these letters as a group, have your night time dreams been affected? Have you noticed your relationship to the passage of time changing? Have you had any deja-vu experiences? Do you find you have an increase in the desire to talk to others about such things? Are you dreaming more about animals and about either dolphins or whales in particular? When you wake up from these dreams, what are you feeling?

17) Do you find yourself called to be in Nature more and less drawn to spend as much time with your technical devices? Are you noticing things in Nature more like the wind, the sky, trees, animals, insects, water, fire, stones, etc.?

18) Do you find during this time of spending time with the letters that you are feeling more compassion for all of life and that compassion is just becoming part of your daily life?

19) Lastly, do you feel the bond you are making with others as you are sharing the impact of these letters is a bond you wish to continue just using the letters as a springboard? If so, what are some of the forms an extension of this bond might take?

Note from author regarding these guidelines:

I am happy to answer any questions about any discussion groups being held in connection with THE DOLPHIN LETTERS. You may email me at: *Muriel@MurielLindsay.com.*

> >